JAMESTOWN EDUCATION

Reading Fluency

Reader's Record

Level
F

Camille L. Z. Blachowicz, Ph.D.

JAMESTOWN EDUCATION

Reading Fluency

Reader's Record

Level
F

Camille L. Z. Blachowicz, Ph.D.

Mc Graw Hill **Glencoe**

New York, New York   Columbus, Ohio   Chicago, Illinois   Peoria, Illinois   Woodland Hills, California

JAMESTOWN 🚢 EDUCATION

Glencoe

The *McGraw·Hill* Companies

Send all inquiries to:
Glencoe/McGraw-Hill
8787 Orion Place
Columbus, OH 43240-4027

ISBN 0-07-845703-3
Printed in the United States of America.
1 2 3 4 5 6 7 8 9 10 021 09 08 07 06 05 04 03

Contents

The passages in this book are taken from the following sources.

How to Use These Books

The Reading Fluency *Reader* contains 72 reading passages. The accompanying *Reader's Record* contains two copies of each of these passages and includes a place for marking *miscues*. You and your partner will take turns using the *Reader*. Each of you will need your own *Reader's Record*. You will also need a stopwatch or a timer.

What Are Miscues?

Miscues are errors or slips that all readers make. These include the following:
- a mispronounced word
- a word substituted for the correct word
- an inserted word
- a skipped word

Repeating a word or correcting oneself immediately is not counted as a miscue.

What Procedure Do I Follow?

1. Work with a partner. One partner is the reader; the other partner is the recorder.

2. Suppose that you are the first to read aloud. Read a selection from the *Reader* as your partner marks any miscues you make on the corresponding page in your *Reader's Record*. The recorder's job is to listen carefully and make a tick mark above each place in the text where a miscue occurs, and to make a slash mark indicating where you stop reading after "Time!" is called.

3. The recorder says when to start and calls "Time!" after a minute.

4. After the reading, the recorder:
   - counts the number of words read, using the number guides at the right-hand side of the passage, and records the Total Words Read
   - writes the total number of miscues for each line in the far right-hand column labeled Miscues. Totals and records the miscues on the Total Errors line
   - subtracts Total Errors from Total Words Read to find the Correct Words Per Minute (WPM) and records that score on the Correct WPM line

5. You review the *Reader's Record*, noting your miscues. Discuss with your partner the characteristics of good reading you have displayed. Then rate your own performance and mark the scale at the bottom of the page.

6. Change roles with your partner and repeat the procedure.

7. You and your partner then begin a second round of reading the same passage. When it is your turn to read, try to improve in pace, expression, and accuracy over the first reading.

8. After completing two readings, record your Correct WPM scores in the back of your *Reader's Record*. Follow the directions on the graph.

1

Fiction

from **"The King of Mazy May"**
by Jack London

First Reading

	Words Read	Miscues

"Mush! Hi! Mush on!" [Walt] cried to the animals, snapping   10   _____
the keen-lashed whip among them.   15   _____

    The dogs sprang against the yoke-straps, and the sled jerked   25   _____
underway so suddenly as to almost throw him off. Then it curved   37   _____
into the creek, poising perilously on one runner. He was almost   48   _____
breathless with suspense, when it finally righted with a bound   58   _____
and sprang ahead again. The creek bank was high and he could   70   _____
not see, although he could hear the cries of the men and knew   83   _____
they were running to cut him off. He did not dare to think what   97   _____
would happen if they caught him; he only clung to the sled, his   110   _____
heart beating wildly, and watched the snow-rim of the bank   120   _____
above him.   122   _____

    Suddenly, over the snow-rim came the flying body of the   132   _____
Irishman, who had leaped straight for the sled in a desperate   143   _____
attempt to capture it; but he was an instant too late. Striking on   156   _____
the very rear of it, he was thrown from his feet, backward, into the   170   _____
snow. Yet, with the quickness of a cat, he had clutched the end of   184   _____
the sled with one hand, turned over, and was dragging behind.   195   _____

Needs Work   1 2 3 4 5   Excellent
Paid attention to punctuation

Needs Work   1 2 3 4 5   Excellent
Sounded good

Total Words Read _____

Total Errors − _____

Correct WPM _____

1

from **"The King of Mazy May"**

by Jack London

	Words Read	Miscues
"Mush! Hi! Mush on!" [Walt] cried to the animals, snapping	10	_____
the keen-lashed whip among them.	15	_____
The dogs sprang against the yoke-straps, and the sled jerked	25	_____
underway so suddenly as to almost throw him off. Then it curved	37	_____
into the creek, poising perilously on one runner. He was almost	48	_____
breathless with suspense, when it finally righted with a bound	58	_____
and sprang ahead again. The creek bank was high and he could	70	_____
not see, although he could hear the cries of the men and knew	83	_____
they were running to cut him off. He did not dare to think what	97	_____
would happen if they caught him; he only clung to the sled, his	110	_____
heart beating wildly, and watched the snow-rim of the bank	120	_____
above him.	122	_____
Suddenly, over the snow-rim came the flying body of the	132	_____
Irishman, who had leaped straight for the sled in a desperate	143	_____
attempt to capture it; but he was an instant too late. Striking on	156	_____
the very rear of it, he was thrown from his feet, backward, into the	170	_____
snow. Yet, with the quickness of a cat, he had clutched the end of	184	_____
the sled with one hand, turned over, and was dragging behind.	195	_____

Needs Work   1 2 3 4 5   Excellent
Paid attention to punctuation

Needs Work   1 2 3 4 5   Excellent
Sounded good

Total Words Read _____

Total Errors − _____

Correct WPM _____

2

Fiction

from "The Summer of the Beautiful White Horse"

by William Saroyan

First Reading

	Words Read	Miscues

⸎

One day back there in the good old days when I was nine and   14   _____

the world was full of every imaginable kind of magnificence, and   25   _____

life was still a delightful and mysterious dream, my cousin Mourad,   36   _____

who was considered crazy by everybody who knew him except   46   _____

me, came to my house at four in the morning and woke me up   60   _____

by tapping on the window of my room.   68   _____

　　Aram, he said.   71   _____

　　I jumped out of bed and looked out the window.   81   _____

　　I couldn't believe what I saw.   87   _____

　　It wasn't morning yet, but it was summer and with daybreak   98   _____

not many minutes around the corner of the world it was light   110   _____

enough for me to know I wasn't dreaming.   118   _____

　　My cousin Mourad was sitting on a beautiful white horse.   128   _____

　　I stuck my head out of the window and rubbed my eyes.   140   _____

　　Yes, he said in Armenian. It's a horse. You're not dreaming.   151   _____

Make it quick if you want to ride.   159   _____

　　I knew my cousin Mourad enjoyed being alive more than   169   _____

anybody else who had ever fallen into the world by mistake, but   181   _____

this was more than even I could believe.   189   _____

　　In the first place, my earliest memories had been memories   199   _____

of horses, and my first longings had been longings to ride.   210   _____

　　This was the wonderful part.   215   _____

Needs Work   1   2   3   4   5   Excellent
Paid attention to punctuation

Needs Work   1   2   3   4   5   Excellent
Sounded good

Total Words Read _____

Total Errors − _____

Correct WPM _____

3

2
Fiction

from "The Summer of the Beautiful White Horse"
by William Saroyan

	Words Read	Miscues

One day back there in the good old days when I was nine and   14   _____

the world was full of every imaginable kind of magnificence, and   25   _____

life was still a delightful and mysterious dream, my cousin Mourad,   36   _____

who was considered crazy by everybody who knew him except   46   _____

me, came to my house at four in the morning and woke me up   60   _____

by tapping on the window of my room.   68   _____

    Aram, he said.   71   _____

    I jumped out of bed and looked out the window.   81   _____

    I couldn't believe what I saw.   87   _____

    It wasn't morning yet, but it was summer and with daybreak   98   _____

not many minutes around the corner of the world it was light   110   _____

enough for me to know I wasn't dreaming.   118   _____

    My cousin Mourad was sitting on a beautiful white horse.   128   _____

    I stuck my head out of the window and rubbed my eyes.   140   _____

    Yes, he said in Armenian. It's a horse. You're not dreaming.   151   _____

Make it quick if you want to ride.   159   _____

    I knew my cousin Mourad enjoyed being alive more than   169   _____

anybody else who had ever fallen into the world by mistake, but   181   _____

this was more than even I could believe.   189   _____

    In the first place, my earliest memories had been memories   199   _____

of horses, and my first longings had been longings to ride.   210   _____

    This was the wonderful part.   215   _____

Needs Work   1   2   3   4   5   Excellent
Paid attention to punctuation

Needs Work   1   2   3   4   5   Excellent
Sounded good

Total Words Read   _____

Total Errors −   _____

Correct WPM   _____

3 Fiction

from *Where the Red Fern Grows*
by Wilson Rawls

First Reading

	Words Read	Miscues

I suppose there's a time in practically every young boy's life | 11 | _____

when he's affected by that wonderful disease of puppy love. | 21 | _____

I don't mean the kind a boy has for the pretty little girl that lives | 36 | _____

down the road. I mean the real kind, the kind that has four small | 50 | _____

feet and a wiggly tail, and sharp little teeth that can gnaw on a | 64 | _____

boy's finger; the kind a boy can romp and play with, even eat | 77 | _____

and sleep with. | 80 | _____

I was ten years old when I first became infected with this | 92 | _____

terrible disease. I'm sure no boy in the world had it worse than | 105 | _____

I did. It's not easy for a young boy to want a dog and not be able | 122 | _____

to have one. It starts gnawing on his heart, and gets all mixed up | 136 | _____

in his dreams. It gets worse and worse, until finally it becomes | 148 | _____

almost unbearable. | 150 | _____

If my dog-wanting had been that of an ordinary boy, I'm sure | 162 | _____

my mother and father would have gotten me a puppy, but my | 174 | _____

wants were different. I didn't want just one dog. I wanted two, | 186 | _____

and not just any kind of dog. They had to be a special kind and | 201 | _____

a special breed. | 204 | _____

Needs Work   1 2 3 4 5   Excellent
Paid attention to punctuation

Needs Work   1 2 3 4 5   Excellent
Sounded good

Total Words Read _____

Total Errors − _____

Correct WPM _____

from ***Where the Red Fern Grows***
by Wilson Rawls

	Words Read	Miscues

I suppose there's a time in practically every young boy's life   11 _____

when he's affected by that wonderful disease of puppy love.   21 _____

I don't mean the kind a boy has for the pretty little girl that lives   36 _____

down the road. I mean the real kind, the kind that has four small   50 _____

feet and a wiggly tail, and sharp little teeth that can gnaw on a   64 _____

boy's finger; the kind a boy can romp and play with, even eat   77 _____

and sleep with.   80 _____

    I was ten years old when I first became infected with this   92 _____

terrible disease. I'm sure no boy in the world had it worse than   105 _____

I did. It's not easy for a young boy to want a dog and not be able   122 _____

to have one. It starts gnawing on his heart, and gets all mixed up   136 _____

in his dreams. It gets worse and worse, until finally it becomes   148 _____

almost unbearable.   150 _____

    If my dog-wanting had been that of an ordinary boy, I'm sure   162 _____

my mother and father would have gotten me a puppy, but my   174 _____

wants were different. I didn't want just one dog. I wanted two,   186 _____

and not just any kind of dog. They had to be a special kind and   201 _____

a special breed.   204 _____

Needs Work   1   2   3   4   5   Excellent
          Paid attention to punctuation

Needs Work   1   2   3   4   5   Excellent
          Sounded good

Total Words Read _____

Total Errors — _____

Correct WPM _____

4 Fiction

from *The Secret Garden*
by Frances Hodgson Burnett

First Reading

	Words Read	Miscues

The robin kept singing and twittering away and tilting his head   11 _____
to one side, as if he were as excited as [Mary] was. What was this   26 _____
under her hands which was square and made of iron and which   38 _____
her fingers found a hole in?   44 _____

It was the lock of the door which had been closed ten years   57 _____
and she put her hand in her pocket, drew out the key and found   71 _____
it fitted the keyhole. She put the key in and turned it. It took two   86 _____
hands to do it, but it did turn.   94 _____

And then she took a long breath and looked behind her up the   107 _____
long walk to see if any one was coming. No one was coming. No   121 _____
one ever did come, it seemed, and she took another long breath,   133 _____
because she could not help it, and she held back the swinging   145 _____
curtain of ivy and pushed back the door which opened slowly—   156 _____
slowly.   157 _____

Then she slipped through it, and shut it behind her, and stood   169 _____
with her back against it, looking about her and breathing quite   180 _____
fast with excitement, and wonder, and delight.   187 _____

She was standing *inside* the secret garden.   194 _____

Needs Work   1   2   3   4   5   Excellent
Paid attention to punctuation

Needs Work   1   2   3   4   5   Excellent
Sounded good

Total Words Read _____

Total Errors − _____

Correct WPM _____

from *The Secret Garden*
by Frances Hodgson Burnett

	Words Read	Miscues
The robin kept singing and twittering away and tilting his head	11	_____
to one side, as if he were as excited as [Mary] was. What was this	26	_____
under her hands which was square and made of iron and which	38	_____
her fingers found a hole in?	44	_____
It was the lock of the door which had been closed ten years	57	_____
and she put her hand in her pocket, drew out the key and found	71	_____
it fitted the keyhole. She put the key in and turned it. It took two	86	_____
hands to do it, but it did turn.	94	_____
And then she took a long breath and looked behind her up the	107	_____
long walk to see if any one was coming. No one was coming. No	121	_____
one ever did come, it seemed, and she took another long breath,	133	_____
because she could not help it, and she held back the swinging	145	_____
curtain of ivy and pushed back the door which opened slowly—	156	_____
slowly.	157	_____
Then she slipped through it, and shut it behind her, and stood	169	_____
with her back against it, looking about her and breathing quite	180	_____
fast with excitement, and wonder, and delight.	187	_____
She was standing *inside* the secret garden.	194	_____

Needs Work   1   2   3   4   5   Excellent
      Paid attention to punctuation

Needs Work   1   2   3   4   5   Excellent
      Sounded good

Total Words Read   _____

Total Errors − _____

Correct WPM   _____

5
Fiction

from *On My Honor*
by Marion Dane Bauer

First Reading

	Words Read	Miscues

"Come on," Tony prodded. "You said out to the sandbar. Are   11   _____
you giving up?"   14   _____

"You sure you'll make it?" Joel eyed his friend's still faintly   25   _____
heaving chest meaningfully. "You look pretty tired to me."   34   _____

Tony gave him a shove, almost caught him off balance. "Swim,"   45   _____
he commanded, and Joel plunged into the water and resumed   55   _____
swimming. Tony started beside him but immediately dropped   63   _____
behind. Joel could hear him, blowing and puffing like a whale.   74   _____

It's not so bad, Joel said to himself, beginning to get his   86   _____
rhythm, discovering the angle that made it possible to keep   96   _____
gaining against the current. Maybe Tony was right and this river   107   _____
swimming would be a good way to practice [for the swim team] . . .   119   _____
now that his father had decided he was old enough to be allowed   132   _____
a bit of freedom.   136   _____

He started the side stroke. He could watch where he was   147   _____
going better that way, keep tabs on how far he still had to go.   161   _____
He couldn't see Tony coming behind, but he didn't need to see   173   _____
him. He could tell he was there, because he sounded like an old   186   _____
paddle wheeler.   188   _____

Only about twenty more feet. Joel caught a toehold in the   199   _____
bottom for a second to look ahead. The water foamed and eddied   211   _____
around the sandbar.   214   _____

Needs Work   1   2   3   4   5   Excellent
Paid attention to punctuation

Needs Work   1   2   3   4   5   Excellent
Sounded good

Total Words Read _____

Total Errors − _____

Correct WPM _____

from *On My Honor*
by Marion Dane Bauer

"Come on," Tony prodded. "You said out to the sandbar. Are	11	_____
you giving up?"	14	_____
"You sure you'll make it?" Joel eyed his friend's still faintly	25	_____
heaving chest meaningfully. "You look pretty tired to me."	34	_____
Tony gave him a shove, almost caught him off balance. "Swim,"	45	_____
he commanded, and Joel plunged into the water and resumed	55	_____
swimming. Tony started beside him but immediately dropped	63	_____
behind. Joel could hear him, blowing and puffing like a whale.	74	_____
It's not so bad, Joel said to himself, beginning to get his	86	_____
rhythm, discovering the angle that made it possible to keep	96	_____
gaining against the current. Maybe Tony was right and this river	107	_____
swimming would be a good way to practice [for the swim team] . . .	119	_____
now that his father had decided he was old enough to be allowed	132	_____
a bit of freedom.	136	_____
He started the side stroke. He could watch where he was	147	_____
going better that way, keep tabs on how far he still had to go.	161	_____
He couldn't see Tony coming behind, but he didn't need to see	173	_____
him. He could tell he was there, because he sounded like an old	186	_____
paddle wheeler.	188	_____
Only about twenty more feet. Joel caught a toehold in the	199	_____
bottom for a second to look ahead. The water foamed and eddied	211	_____
around the sandbar.	214	_____

Needs Work   1 2 3 4 5   Excellent
Paid attention to punctuation

Needs Work   1 2 3 4 5   Excellent
Sounded good

Total Words Read _____

Total Errors − _____

Correct WPM _____

6
Nonfiction

from *Pioneer Girl:*
Growing Up on the Prairie
by Andrea Warren

First Reading

	Words Read	Miscues

The blizzard of '88 came to be known as the Schoolchildren's | 11 | _____

Blizzard, since many children were in school when it struck. | 21 | _____

Some had not even worn coats that warm winter day. Then the | 33 | _____

wind changed suddenly and clouds came rolling in like thick | 43 | _____

bales of cotton, driving heavy snow in their wake. Quickly the | 54 | _____

water turned freezing cold. Farmers in the fields struggled to | 64 | _____

get back to their houses. Animals suffocated or froze under the | 75 | _____

raging snow. | 77 | _____

Schoolhouses were usually not built very well and often | 86 | _____

had little fuel on hand. Most schoolteachers were teenage girls. | 96 | _____

Some became frantic. They had to decide whether to stay in the | 108 | _____

schoolhouse overnight, knowing they might freeze, or try to get | 118 | _____

the children home without getting lost. Many who survived the | 128 | _____

night in their schools burned the desks to stay warm. | 138 | _____

The storm was most dangerous on open prairies, but some | 148 | _____

townspeople froze to death when they got caught outside in | 158 | _____

the storm's whiteout. The newspapers reported that in Hastings, | 167 | _____

Nebraska, a blind college professor was the hero of the blizzard. | 178 | _____

He did not become disoriented in the storm as sighted people | 189 | _____

did, so he was able to get to the local school. He had the children | 204 | _____

form a human chain and managed to get every child safely home. | 216 | _____

Needs Work   1   2   3   4   5   Excellent
Paid attention to punctuation

Needs Work   1   2   3   4   5   Excellent
Sounded good

Total Words Read _____

Total Errors − _____

Correct WPM _____

6
Nonfiction

from *Pioneer Girl:*
Growing Up on the Prairie
by Andrea Warren

	Words Read	Miscues

The blizzard of '88 came to be known as the Schoolchildren's | 11 | _____
Blizzard, since many children were in school when it struck. | 21 | _____
Some had not even worn coats that warm winter day. Then the | 33 | _____
wind changed suddenly and clouds came rolling in like thick | 43 | _____
bales of cotton, driving heavy snow in their wake. Quickly the | 54 | _____
water turned freezing cold. Farmers in the fields struggled to | 64 | _____
get back to their houses. Animals suffocated or froze under the | 75 | _____
raging snow. | 77 | _____

Schoolhouses were usually not built very well and often | 86 | _____
had little fuel on hand. Most schoolteachers were teenage girls. | 96 | _____
Some became frantic. They had to decide whether to stay in the | 108 | _____
schoolhouse overnight, knowing they might freeze, or try to get | 118 | _____
the children home without getting lost. Many who survived the | 128 | _____
night in their schools burned the desks to stay warm. | 138 | _____

The storm was most dangerous on open prairies, but some | 148 | _____
townspeople froze to death when they got caught outside in | 158 | _____
the storm's whiteout. The newspapers reported that in Hastings, | 167 | _____
Nebraska, a blind college professor was the hero of the blizzard. | 178 | _____
He did not become disoriented in the storm as sighted people | 189 | _____
did, so he was able to get to the local school. He had the children | 204 | _____
form a human chain and managed to get every child safely home. | 216 | _____

Needs Work   1   2   3   4   5   Excellent
Paid attention to punctuation

Needs Work   1   2   3   4   5   Excellent
Sounded good

Total Words Read _____

Total Errors − _____

Correct WPM _____

7
Nonfiction

from *Out of Darkness:*
The Story of Louis Braille
by Russell Freedman

First Reading

	Words Read	Miscues

The dormitory was dark and still. Only one boy was still — 11 — _____
awake. He sat on the edge of his bed at a far corner of the room, — 27 — _____
holding a writing board and a sheet of thick paper on his lap. — 40 — _____
Working slowly, deliberately, he punched tiny holes across the — 49 — _____
page with the sharp point of a stylus. Every so often, he paused — 62 — _____
and ran his fingers across the raised dots on the opposite side — 74 — _____
of the paper. Then he continued working with his stylus. — 84 — _____

He was interrupted by a husky whisper coming from the — 94 — _____
next bed. The same hushed conversation took place almost every — 104 — _____
night—the same questions, the same answers. — 111 — _____

"Louis? That you? Still punching dots?" — 117 — _____

"Shh! Be quiet, Gabriel. It's late. You'll wake up everyone." — 127 — _____

"You'd better quit and get some rest, Louis. The director will — 138 — _____
be furious if you doze off in class again." — 147 — _____

"I know. I know. I'm almost finished now. Go back to sleep!" — 159 — _____

Louis Braille placed his paper and stylus on a shelf behind his — 171 — _____
bed. Extending his arm before him, he walked across the dormitory — 182 — _____
and stood before an open window. He was a thin, handsome boy — 194 — _____
with the strong features of his French ancestors. Tangled blond — 204 — _____
hair fell across his forehead. His eyes, tinged with purple, stared — 215 — _____
blankly from above prominent cheekbones. — 220 — _____

Needs Work   1   2   3   4   5   Excellent
Paid attention to punctuation

Needs Work   1   2   3   4   5   Excellent
Sounded good

Total Words Read _____

Total Errors − _____

Correct WPM _____

from *Out of Darkness:*
The Story of Louis Braille
by Russell Freedman

Second Reading

	Words Read	Miscues

The dormitory was dark and still. Only one boy was still | 11 | _____

awake. He sat on the edge of his bed at a far corner of the room, | 27 | _____

holding a writing board and a sheet of thick paper on his lap. | 40 | _____

Working slowly, deliberately, he punched tiny holes across the | 49 | _____

page with the sharp point of a stylus. Every so often, he paused | 62 | _____

and ran his fingers across the raised dots on the opposite side | 74 | _____

of the paper. Then he continued working with his stylus. | 84 | _____

He was interrupted by a husky whisper coming from the | 94 | _____

next bed. The same hushed conversation took place almost every | 104 | _____

night—the same questions, the same answers. | 111 | _____

"Louis? That you? Still punching dots?" | 117 | _____

"Shh! Be quiet, Gabriel. It's late. You'll wake up everyone." | 127 | _____

"You'd better quit and get some rest, Louis. The director will | 138 | _____

be furious if you doze off in class again." | 147 | _____

"I know. I know. I'm almost finished now. Go back to sleep!" | 159 | _____

Louis Braille placed his paper and stylus on a shelf behind his | 171 | _____

bed. Extending his arm before him, he walked across the dormitory | 182 | _____

and stood before an open window. He was a thin, handsome boy | 194 | _____

with the strong features of his French ancestors. Tangled blond | 204 | _____

hair fell across his forehead. His eyes, tinged with purple, stared | 215 | _____

blankly from above prominent cheekbones. | 220 | _____

Needs Work 1 2 3 4 5 Excellent
Paid attention to punctuation

Needs Work 1 2 3 4 5 Excellent
Sounded good

Total Words Read _____

Total Errors − _____

Correct WPM _____

8
Fiction

from **"The Horse of the Sword"**
by Manuel Buaken

First Reading

	Words Read	Miscues

~~~~~~~~

	Words Read	Miscues
"Boy, get rid of that horse," said one of the wise old men	13	_____
from Abra where the racing horses thrive on the good Bermuda	24	_____
grass. . . . "That's a bandit's horse. See that Sign of Evil on him.	36	_____
Something tragic will happen to you if you keep him."	46	_____
But another one of the old horse traders who had gathered at	58	_____
that auction declared: "That's a good omen. The Sword he bears	69	_____
on his shoulder means leadership and power. He's a true mount	80	_____
for a chieftain. He's a free man's fighting horse."	89	_____
As for me, I knew this gray colt was a wonder horse the moment	103	_____
I saw him. These other people were blind. They only saw that this	116	_____
gray, shaggy horse bore the marks of many whips, that his ribs	128	_____
almost stuck through his mangy hide, that his great eyes rolled	139	_____
in defiance and fear as the auctioneer approached him. They	149	_____
couldn't see the meaning of that Sword he bore—a marking not	161	_____
in the color, which was a uniform gray, but in the way that the	175	_____
hair had arranged itself permanently: it was parted to form an	186	_____
outline of a sword that was broad on his neck and tapered to	199	_____
a fine point on his shoulder.	205	_____

Needs Work   1   2   3   4   5   Excellent
Paid attention to punctuation

Needs Work   1   2   3   4   5   Excellent
Sounded good

Total Words Read _____

Total Errors − _____

Correct WPM _____

from "The Horse of the Sword"

by Manuel Buaken

	Words Read	Miscues

"Boy, get rid of that horse," said one of the wise old men | 13 | _____

from Abra where the racing horses thrive on the good Bermuda | 24 | _____

grass. . . . "That's a bandit's horse. See that Sign of Evil on him. | 36 | _____

Something tragic will happen to you if you keep him." | 46 | _____

But another one of the old horse traders who had gathered at | 58 | _____

that auction declared: "That's a good omen. The Sword he bears | 69 | _____

on his shoulder means leadership and power. He's a true mount | 80 | _____

for a chieftain. He's a free man's fighting horse." | 89 | _____

As for me, I knew this gray colt was a wonder horse the moment | 103 | _____

I saw him. These other people were blind. They only saw that this | 116 | _____

gray, shaggy horse bore the marks of many whips, that his ribs | 128 | _____

almost stuck through his mangy hide, that his great eyes rolled | 139 | _____

in defiance and fear as the auctioneer approached him. They | 149 | _____

couldn't see the meaning of that Sword he bore—a marking not | 161 | _____

in the color, which was a uniform gray, but in the way that the | 175 | _____

hair had arranged itself permanently: it was parted to form an | 186 | _____

outline of a sword that was broad on his neck and tapered to | 199 | _____

a fine point on his shoulder. | 205 | _____

Needs Work   1   2   3   4   5   Excellent
Paid attention to punctuation

Needs Work   1   2   3   4   5   Excellent
Sounded good

Total Words Read _____

Total Errors – _____

Correct WPM _____

9

Fiction

from "The Drover's Wife"
by Henry Lawson

First Reading

	Words Read	Miscues

∝∝∝

Four ragged, dried-up-looking children are playing about the | 8 | _____

house. Suddenly one of them yells: "Snake! Mother, here's a snake!" | 19 | _____

The gaunt, sun-browned bushwoman dashes from the kitchen, | 27 | _____

snatches her baby from the ground, holds it on her left hip, and | 40 | _____

reaches for a stick. | 44 | _____

"Where is it?" | 47 | _____

"Here! Gone into the wood-heap!" yells the eldest boy— | 56 | _____

a sharp-faced, excited urchin of eleven. "Stop there, mother! | 65 | _____

I'll have him. Stand back! I'll have the beggar!" | 74 | _____

"Tommy, come here, or you'll be bit. Come here at once when | 86 | _____

I tell you, you little wretch!" | 92 | _____

The youngster comes reluctantly, carrying a stick bigger than | 101 | _____

himself. Then he yells, triumphantly: | 106 | _____

"There it goes—under the house!" and darts away with club | 117 | _____

uplifted. At the same time the big, black, yellow-eyed dog-of-all- | 127 | _____

breeds, who has shown the wildest interest in the proceedings, | 136 | _____

breaks his chain and rushes after that snake. He is a moment late, | 149 | _____

however, and his nose reaches the crack in the slabs just as the | 162 | _____

end of its tail disappears. Almost at the same moment the boy's | 174 | _____

club comes down and skins the aforesaid nose. Alligator [the dog] | 185 | _____

takes small notice of this, and proceeds to undermine the | 195 | _____

building; but he is subdued after a struggle and chained up. | 206 | _____

They cannot afford to lose him. | 212 | _____

Needs Work   1   2   3   4   5   Excellent
Paid attention to punctuation

Needs Work   1   2   3   4   5   Excellent
Sounded good

Total Words Read   _____

Total Errors   −   _____

Correct WPM   _____

17

9

Fiction

from "The Drover's Wife"

by Henry Lawson

	Words Read	Miscues

Four ragged, dried-up-looking children are playing about the
house. Suddenly one of them yells: "Snake! Mother, here's a snake!"

The gaunt, sun-browned bushwoman dashes from the kitchen,
snatches her baby from the ground, holds it on her left hip, and
reaches for a stick.

"Where is it?"

"Here! Gone into the wood-heap!" yells the eldest boy—
a sharp-faced, excited urchin of eleven. "Stop there, mother!
I'll have him. Stand back! I'll have the beggar!"

"Tommy, come here, or you'll be bit. Come here at once when
I tell you, you little wretch!"

The youngster comes reluctantly, carrying a stick bigger than
himself. Then he yells, triumphantly:

"There it goes—under the house!" and darts away with club
uplifted. At the same time the big, black, yellow-eyed dog-of-all-
breeds, who has shown the wildest interest in the proceedings,
breaks his chain and rushes after that snake. He is a moment late,
however, and his nose reaches the crack in the slabs just as the
end of its tail disappears. Almost at the same moment the boy's
club comes down and skins the aforesaid nose. Alligator [the dog]
takes small notice of this, and proceeds to undermine the
building; but he is subdued after a struggle and chained up.
They cannot afford to lose him.

Words Read
8
19
27
40
44
47
56
65
74
86
92
101
106
117
127
136
149
162
174
185
195
206
212

Needs Work 1 2 3 4 5 Excellent

Paid attention to punctuation

Needs Work 1 2 3 4 5 Excellent

Sounded good

Total Words Read _____

Total Errors − _____

Correct WPM _____

18

A Fighter for Justice

10

Nonfiction

	Words Read	Miscues

He was denied admission to one law school because he was   11 _____

African American. But today that same school has a law library   22 _____

named after him. You may not know much about Thurgood   32 _____

Marshall, but he strengthened education rights for African   40 _____

Americans all over the United States.   46 _____

Marshall was born in Baltimore in 1908. Like other African   56 _____

American students of his time, he went to segregated schools.   66 _____

These schools were not illegal. An 1896 law stated that schools   77 _____

for African Americans could be "separate but equal." But Marshall   87 _____

knew that most African American schools were not equal to those   98 _____

of whites. He decided to do something about it.   107 _____

Marshall received a law degree from Howard University. Then   116 _____

he began to work at changing the country's schools. In 1935 he   128 _____

successfully sued the University of Maryland Law School to   137 _____

accept its first African American student. Other cases followed,   146 _____

with similar results.   149 _____

By the 1950s, Marshall was ready to turn to grade schools   160 _____

and high schools. In 1954 he accepted the case of Linda Brown,   172 _____

who wanted to attend a white grade school near her home. As a   185 _____

result of Marshall's arguments, the Supreme Court changed the law.   195 _____

In 1967 Marshall became the first African American appointed   204 _____

to the U.S. Supreme Court. Until he retired in 1991, he supported   216 _____

many other civil rights bills.   221 _____

Needs Work   1   2   3   4   5   Excellent
Paid attention to punctuation

Needs Work   1   2   3   4   5   Excellent
Sounded good

Total Words Read _____

Total Errors − _____

Correct WPM _____

A Fighter for Justice

Second Reading

	Words Read	Miscues

He was denied admission to one law school because he was   11 _____

African American. But today that same school has a law library   22 _____

named after him. You may not know much about Thurgood   32 _____

Marshall, but he strengthened education rights for African   40 _____

Americans all over the United States.   46 _____

    Marshall was born in Baltimore in 1908. Like other African   56 _____

American students of his time, he went to segregated schools.   66 _____

These schools were not illegal. An 1896 law stated that schools   77 _____

for African Americans could be "separate but equal." But Marshall   87 _____

knew that most African American schools were not equal to those   98 _____

of whites. He decided to do something about it.   107 _____

    Marshall received a law degree from Howard University. Then   116 _____

he began to work at changing the country's schools. In 1935 he   128 _____

successfully sued the University of Maryland Law School to   137 _____

accept its first African American student. Other cases followed,   146 _____

with similar results.   149 _____

    By the 1950s, Marshall was ready to turn to grade schools   160 _____

and high schools. In 1954 he accepted the case of Linda Brown,   172 _____

who wanted to attend a white grade school near her home. As a   185 _____

result of Marshall's arguments, the Supreme Court changed the law.   195 _____

    In 1967 Marshall became the first African American appointed   204 _____

to the U.S. Supreme Court. Until he retired in 1991, he supported   216 _____

many other civil rights bills.   221 _____

Needs Work 1 2 3 4 5 Excellent
Paid attention to punctuation

Needs Work 1 2 3 4 5 Excellent
Sounded good

Total Words Read _____

Total Errors − _____

Correct WPM _____

11

Nonfiction

from *Living up the Street*
by Gary Soto

	Words Read	Miscues

First Reading

	Words Read	Miscues
I cut another bunch, then another, fighting the snap and	10	_____
whip of vines. After ten minutes of groping for grapes, my first	22	_____
pan brimmed with bunches. I poured them on the paper tray,	33	_____
which was bordered by a wooden frame that kept the grapes from	45	_____
rolling off, and they spilled like jewels from a pirate's chest. The	57	_____
tray was only half filled, so I hurried to jump under the vines and	71	_____
begin groping, cutting, and tugging at the grapes again. I emptied	82	_____
the pan, raked the grapes with my hands to make them look like	95	_____
they filled the tray, and jumped back under the vine on my knees.	108	_____
I tried to cut faster because Mother, in the next row, was slowly	121	_____
moving ahead. I peeked into her row and saw five trays gleaming	133	_____
in the early morning. I cut, pulled hard, and stopped to gather the	146	_____
grapes that missed the pan; already bored, I spat on a few to wash	160	_____
them before tossing them like popcorn into my mouth.	169	_____
So it went. Two pans equaled one tray—or six cents. By	181	_____
lunchtime I had a trail of thirty-seven trays behind me while	192	_____
Mother had sixty or more. We met about halfway from our last	204	_____
trays, and I sat down with a grunt, knees wet from kneeling on	217	_____
dropped grapes.	219	_____

Needs Work 1 2 3 4 5 Excellent
Paid attention to punctuation

Needs Work 1 2 3 4 5 Excellent
Sounded good

Total Words Read _____

Total Errors – _____

Correct WPM _____

from *Living up the Street*
by Gary Soto

	Words Read	Miscues
I cut another bunch, then another, fighting the snap and	10	_____
whip of vines. After ten minutes of groping for grapes, my first	22	_____
pan brimmed with bunches. I poured them on the paper tray,	33	_____
which was bordered by a wooden frame that kept the grapes from	45	_____
rolling off, and they spilled like jewels from a pirate's chest. The	57	_____
tray was only half filled, so I hurried to jump under the vines and	71	_____
begin groping, cutting, and tugging at the grapes again. I emptied	82	_____
the pan, raked the grapes with my hands to make them look like	95	_____
they filled the tray, and jumped back under the vine on my knees.	108	_____
I tried to cut faster because Mother, in the next row, was slowly	121	_____
moving ahead. I peeked into her row and saw five trays gleaming	133	_____
in the early morning. I cut, pulled hard, and stopped to gather the	146	_____
grapes that missed the pan; already bored, I spat on a few to wash	160	_____
them before tossing them like popcorn into my mouth.	169	_____
So it went. Two pans equaled one tray—or six cents. By	181	_____
lunchtime I had a trail of thirty-seven trays behind me while	192	_____
Mother had sixty or more. We met about halfway from our last	204	_____
trays, and I sat down with a grunt, knees wet from kneeling on	217	_____
dropped grapes.	219	_____

Needs Work   1 2 3 4 5   Excellent
Paid attention to punctuation

Needs Work   1 2 3 4 5   Excellent
Sounded good

Total Words Read   _____

Total Errors − _____

Correct WPM   _____

12
Nonfiction

from *My Indian Boyhood*
by Luther Standing Bear

First Reading

	Words Read	Miscues

Away I went, my little pony putting all he had into the race. — 13 _____

It was not long before I lost sight of father, but I kept going just — 28 _____

the same. I threw my blanket back, and the chill of the autumn — 41 _____

morning struck my body, but I did not mind. On I went. It was — 55 _____

wonderful to race over the ground with all these horsemen — 65 _____

about me. There was no shouting, no noise of any kind except the — 78 _____

pounding of the horses' feet. The herd was now running and had — 90 _____

raised a cloud of dust. I felt no fear until we had entered this — 104 _____

cloud of dust and I could see nothing about me—only hear the — 117 _____

sound of feet. Where was father? Where was I going? On I rode — 130 _____

through the cloud, for I knew I must keep going. — 140 _____

Then all at once I realized that I was in the midst of the — 154 _____

buffalo, their dark bodies rushing all about me and their great — 165 _____

heads moving up and down to the sound of their hoofs beating — 177 _____

upon the earth. Then it was that fear overcame me and I leaned — 190 _____

close down upon my little pony's body and clutched him tightly. — 201 _____

I can never tell you how I felt. — 209 _____

Needs Work 1 2 3 4 5 Excellent
Paid attention to punctuation

Needs Work 1 2 3 4 5 Excellent
Sounded good

Total Words Read _____

Total Errors − _____

Correct WPM _____

12

Nonfiction

from *My Indian Boyhood*
by Luther Standing Bear

	Words Read	Miscues

Away I went, my little pony putting all he had into the race. | 13 | _____
It was not long before I lost sight of father, but I kept going just | 28 | _____
the same. I threw my blanket back, and the chill of the autumn | 41 | _____
morning struck my body, but I did not mind. On I went. It was | 55 | _____
wonderful to race over the ground with all these horsemen | 65 | _____
about me. There was no shouting, no noise of any kind except the | 78 | _____
pounding of the horses' feet. The herd was now running and had | 90 | _____
raised a cloud of dust. I felt no fear until we had entered this | 104 | _____
cloud of dust and I could see nothing about me—only hear the | 117 | _____
sound of feet. Where was father? Where was I going? On I rode | 130 | _____
through the cloud, for I knew I must keep going. | 140 | _____

Then all at once I realized that I was in the midst of the | 154 | _____
buffalo, their dark bodies rushing all about me and their great | 165 | _____
heads moving up and down to the sound of their hoofs beating | 177 | _____
upon the earth. Then it was that fear overcame me and I leaned | 190 | _____
close down upon my little pony's body and clutched him tightly. | 201 | _____
I can never tell you how I felt. | 209 | _____

Needs Work   1   2   3   4   5   Excellent
Paid attention to punctuation

Needs Work   1   2   3   4   5   Excellent
Sounded good

Total Words Read _____

Total Errors − _____

Correct WPM _____

from *The Dolphins and Me*
by Don C. Reed

Nonfiction

	Words Read	Miscues

Not wanting to dangle my legs in the water, I stood awkwardly | 12 | _____

on one foot at a time as I fumbled into the big, flopping swimfins. | 26 | _____

As I pulled the black plastic mask over my face, the strap | 38 | _____

tugged at my hair. When I opened my eyes, my field of vision | 51 | _____

was narrowed by the mask. It was like staring through a section | 63 | _____

of pipe. | 65 | _____

I took one giant step forward and fell . . . into another world. | 76 | _____

I heard the crash of the surface as it broke apart and thumped | 89 | _____

shut above me; I felt the massage of pressure and the cold water | 102 | _____

rushing down my neck and spine. Air bubbles slid ticklingly up | 113 | _____

my face, heading for the surface, while I headed the opposite | 124 | _____

way, falling, dragged down by the heavy lead work belt around | 135 | _____

my waist. | 137 | _____

As the bubbles of my entry cleared, my vision returned. My | 148 | _____

fintips folded softly underneath me as I landed on the green, | 159 | _____

algae-covered floor. | 161 | _____

Oddly, I didn't spot the dolphins right away. Perhaps their | 171 | _____

dark/light camouflage patterns broke up their outlines. Then, all | 180 | _____

at once, there they were—and so much *bigger* than I had expected. | 193 | _____

Needs Work   1   2   3   4   5   Excellent
Paid attention to punctuation

Needs Work   1   2   3   4   5   Excellent
Sounded good

Total Words Read _____

Total Errors − _____

Correct WPM _____

13 Nonfiction

from *The Dolphins and Me*
by Don C. Reed

	Words Read	Miscues

Not wanting to dangle my legs in the water, I stood awkwardly | 12 | _____

on one foot at a time as I fumbled into the big, flopping swimfins. | 26 | _____

As I pulled the black plastic mask over my face, the strap | 38 | _____

tugged at my hair. When I opened my eyes, my field of vision | 51 | _____

was narrowed by the mask. It was like staring through a section | 63 | _____

of pipe. | 65 | _____

I took one giant step forward and fell . . . into another world. | 76 | _____

I heard the crash of the surface as it broke apart and thumped | 89 | _____

shut above me; I felt the massage of pressure and the cold water | 102 | _____

rushing down my neck and spine. Air bubbles slid ticklingly up | 113 | _____

my face, heading for the surface, while I headed the opposite | 124 | _____

way, falling, dragged down by the heavy lead work belt around | 135 | _____

my waist. | 137 | _____

As the bubbles of my entry cleared, my vision returned. My | 148 | _____

fintips folded softly underneath me as I landed on the green, | 159 | _____

algae-covered floor. | 161 | _____

Oddly, I didn't spot the dolphins right away. Perhaps their | 171 | _____

dark/light camouflage patterns broke up their outlines. Then, all | 180 | _____

at once, there they were—and so much *bigger* than I had expected. | 193 | _____

Needs Work 1 2 3 4 5 Excellent
Paid attention to punctuation

Needs Work 1 2 3 4 5 Excellent
Sounded good

Total Words Read _____

Total Errors − _____

Correct WPM _____

14
Fiction

from *Old Yeller*
by Fred Gipson

	Words Read	Miscues
First Reading

    It was while Papa and I were cutting wild hay in a little patch   14 _____
of prairie back of the house. A big diamondback rattler struck at   26 _____
Papa and Papa chopped his head off with one quick lick of his   39 _____
scythe. The head dropped to the ground three or four feet away   51 _____
from the writhing body. It lay there, with the ugly mouth opening   63 _____
and shutting, still trying to bite something.   70 _____

    As smart as Bell was, you'd have thought he'd have better   81 _____
sense than to go up and nuzzle that rattler's head. But he didn't,   94 _____
and a second later, he was falling back, howling and slinging his   106 _____
own head till his ears popped. But it was too late then. That   119 _____
snake mouth had snapped shut on his nose, driving the fangs in   131 _____
so deep that it was a full minute before he could sling the bloody   145 _____
head loose.   147 _____

    He died that night, and I cried for a week. Papa tried to make   161 _____
me feel better by promising to get me another dog right away, but   174 _____
I wouldn't have it. It made me mad just to think about some   187 _____
other dog's trying to take Bell's place.   194 _____

    And I still felt the same about it.   202 _____

Needs Work   1 2 3 4 5   Excellent
     Paid attention to punctuation

Needs Work   1 2 3 4 5   Excellent
     Sounded good

Total Words Read _____

Total Errors − _____

Correct WPM _____

from *Old Yeller*
by Fred Gipson

It was while Papa and I were cutting wild hay in a little patch **14** _____

of prairie back of the house. A big diamondback rattler struck at **26** _____

Papa and Papa chopped his head off with one quick lick of his **39** _____

scythe. The head dropped to the ground three or four feet away **51** _____

from the writhing body. It lay there, with the ugly mouth opening **63** _____

and shutting, still trying to bite something. **70** _____

As smart as Bell was, you'd have thought he'd have better **81** _____

sense than to go up and nuzzle that rattler's head. But he didn't, **94** _____

and a second later, he was falling back, howling and slinging his **106** _____

own head till his ears popped. But it was too late then. That **119** _____

snake mouth had snapped shut on his nose, driving the fangs in **131** _____

so deep that it was a full minute before he could sling the bloody **145** _____

head loose. **147** _____

He died that night, and I cried for a week. Papa tried to make **161** _____

me feel better by promising to get me another dog right away, but **174** _____

I wouldn't have it. It made me mad just to think about some **187** _____

other dog's trying to take Bell's place. **194** _____

And I still felt the same about it. **202** _____

Needs Work   1   2   3   4   5   Excellent
Paid attention to punctuation

Needs Work   1   2   3   4   5   Excellent
Sounded good

Total Words Read _____

Total Errors − _____

Correct WPM _____

15 Raven and the Haida People

Nonfiction

First Reading

	Words Read	Miscues

People have always told stories that explain how the world   10 _____

came to be and how people arrived on it. On the Northwest   22 _____

Coast of North America, Native Americans tell about Raven.   31 _____

Raven is a giant bird who can change himself into human form   43 _____

by pushing up his beak and shrugging off his wings, which then   55 _____

become a cloak. The stories also assure the people that Raven   66 _____

takes special care of those who venerate him.   74 _____

According to tradition, the universe always existed as a wide   84 _____

ocean that covered swampy ground. Birds and sea creatures lived   94 _____

in and around it. Raven made the earth by scooping up pebbles   106 _____

with his beak and dropping them into the ocean. When the earth   118 _____

was big enough, Raven swooped down and walked on the shore,   129 _____

looking out at the vast ocean and feeling lonely.   138 _____

Then he began to hear tiny voices. They seemed to be coming   150 _____

from a clam shell at his feet. Raven pried open the clam shell with   164 _____

his mighty claws and peered in. Inside the clam shell were people.   176 _____

As the story goes, Raven coaxed them out of the shell and set   189 _____

them on land, and they were the first people of the Haida tribe   202 _____

of the Northwest Coast.   206 _____

Needs Work   1   2   3   4   5   Excellent
_____
Paid attention to punctuation

Needs Work   1   2   3   4   5   Excellent
_____
Sounded good

Total Words Read _____

Total Errors − _____

Correct WPM _____

Raven and the Haida People

	Words Read	Miscues

People have always told stories that explain how the world `10` _____

came to be and how people arrived on it. On the Northwest `22` _____

Coast of North America, Native Americans tell about Raven. `31` _____

Raven is a giant bird who can change himself into human form `43` _____

by pushing up his beak and shrugging off his wings, which then `55` _____

become a cloak. The stories also assure the people that Raven `66` _____

takes special care of those who venerate him. `74` _____

According to tradition, the universe always existed as a wide `84` _____

ocean that covered swampy ground. Birds and sea creatures lived `94` _____

in and around it. Raven made the earth by scooping up pebbles `106` _____

with his beak and dropping them into the ocean. When the earth `118` _____

was big enough, Raven swooped down and walked on the shore, `129` _____

looking out at the vast ocean and feeling lonely. `138` _____

Then he began to hear tiny voices. They seemed to be coming `150` _____

from a clam shell at his feet. Raven pried open the clam shell with `164` _____

his mighty claws and peered in. Inside the clam shell were people. `176` _____

As the story goes, Raven coaxed them out of the shell and set `189` _____

them on land, and they were the first people of the Haida tribe `202` _____

of the Northwest Coast. `206` _____

Needs Work   1   2   3   4   5   Excellent
Paid attention to punctuation

Needs Work   1   2   3   4   5   Excellent
Sounded good

Total Words Read _____

Total Errors − _____

Correct WPM _____

16
Nonfiction

from *First in Their Hearts:*
A Biography of George Washington
by Thomas Fleming

First Reading

	Words Read	Miscues

Washington was a leader. A leader must make such hard, — 10 _____

heartbreaking decisions. Those who follow, who serve in the — 19 _____

ranks, forget the loneliness of those at the helm, but there are — 31 _____

times when they are all too grateful for their presence. A year — 43 _____

after [Major] André's death, Washington and a group of French — 53 _____

officers visited West Point and decided to return by boat to — 64 _____

headquarters at New Windsor, some five miles upstream. It was — 74 _____

winter, and the river was full of rushing, cracking ice. The wind — 86 _____

began to blow hard, and the Hudson's formidable waves crashed — 96 _____

over the bow. As they neared their rocky landing place, there was — 108 _____

a veritable surf running. The master of the oarsmen lost his nerve — 120 _____

and swore the wallowing boat was going down. Panic swept the — 131 _____

passengers until Washington put out his big hand. "Courage, my — 141 _____

friends," he called. "I will steer. My place is at the helm." With — 154 _____

skill undoubtedly derived from many hours on his native — 163 _____

Potomac, he landed them safely. — 168 _____

This fatherly spirit grew steadily in Washington as the war — 178 _____

progressed. In his youth, he had been helped by older men. — 189 _____

As commander-in-chief, he returned the generosity tenfold. — 196 _____

Needs Work   1   2   3   4   5   Excellent
Paid attention to punctuation

Needs Work   1   2   3   4   5   Excellent
Sounded good

Total Words Read _____

Total Errors − _____

Correct WPM _____

from *First in Their Hearts:*
A Biography of George Washington
by Thomas Fleming

Washington was a leader. A leader must make such hard,	10	_____
heartbreaking decisions. Those who follow, who serve in the	19	_____
ranks, forget the loneliness of those at the helm, but there are	31	_____
times when they are all too grateful for their presence. A year	43	_____
after [Major] André's death, Washington and a group of French	53	_____
officers visited West Point and decided to return by boat to	64	_____
headquarters at New Windsor, some five miles upstream. It was	74	_____
winter, and the river was full of rushing, cracking ice. The wind	86	_____
began to blow hard, and the Hudson's formidable waves crashed	96	_____
over the bow. As they neared their rocky landing place, there was	108	_____
a veritable surf running. The master of the oarsmen lost his nerve	120	_____
and swore the wallowing boat was going down. Panic swept the	131	_____
passengers until Washington put out his big hand. "Courage, my	141	_____
friends," he called. "I will steer. My place is at the helm." With	154	_____
skill undoubtedly derived from many hours on his native	163	_____
Potomac, he landed them safely.	168	_____
This fatherly spirit grew steadily in Washington as the war	178	_____
progressed. In his youth, he had been helped by older men.	189	_____
As commander-in-chief, he returned the generosity tenfold.	196	_____

Needs Work 1 2 3 4 5 Excellent
Paid attention to punctuation

Needs Work 1 2 3 4 5 Excellent
Sounded good

Total Words Read _____

Total Errors – _____

Correct WPM _____

17

Nonfiction

A Monument to America

First Reading

	Words Read	Miscues

〜〜〜

The American artist Gutzon Borglum grew up on the frontier — 10 _____

and got used to its vast open spaces. The son of a Danish immigrant, — 24 _____

Borglum loved America deeply. — 28 _____

Borglum wanted to do something really important. He — 36 _____

believed that the power of America came from its ability to — 47 _____

think big thoughts and to dare to do great deeds. In 1923 he — 60 _____

got the chance he had been waiting for. A state official in South — 73 _____

Dakota was looking for someone to carve a monument into the — 84 _____

side of Mount Rushmore in the Black Hills. — 92 _____

Borglum jumped at the chance. He suggested that he carve the — 103 _____

heads of two presidents, Abraham Lincoln and George Washington. — 112 _____

Later he would add Thomas Jefferson and Theodore Roosevelt. — 121 _____

The task was enormous. First, Borglum carved four five-foot- — 130 _____

high heads to serve as models. Each head on the actual monument — 141 _____

would be 60 feet high. — 146 _____

Then Borglum had workers dynamite the mountain in — 154 _____

carefully selected places. — 157 _____

The next task was to sculpt the faces out of the rough granite — 170 _____

shapes created by the dynamite blasts. Borglum supervised miners — 179 _____

who used drills, hammers, and chisels to shape and smooth the — 190 _____

granite stone. Slowly the faces of the four presidents emerged. — 200 _____

In 1941 the massive work of art was completed. The job had — 212 _____

taken 14 years and had cost just under $1 million. — 222 _____

Needs Work   1 2 3 4 5   Excellent
Paid attention to punctuation

Needs Work   1 2 3 4 5   Excellent
Sounded good

Total Words Read _____

Total Errors − _____

Correct WPM _____

A Monument to America

	Words Read	Miscues

The American artist Gutzon Borglum grew up on the frontier   10 _____

and got used to its vast open spaces. The son of a Danish immigrant,   24 _____

Borglum loved America deeply.   28 _____

Borglum wanted to do something really important. He   36 _____

believed that the power of America came from its ability to   47 _____

think big thoughts and to dare to do great deeds. In 1923 he   60 _____

got the chance he had been waiting for. A state official in South   73 _____

Dakota was looking for someone to carve a monument into the   84 _____

side of Mount Rushmore in the Black Hills.   92 _____

Borglum jumped at the chance. He suggested that he carve the   103 _____

heads of two presidents, Abraham Lincoln and George Washington.   112 _____

Later he would add Thomas Jefferson and Theodore Roosevelt.   121 _____

The task was enormous. First, Borglum carved four five-foot-   130 _____

high heads to serve as models. Each head on the actual monument   141 _____

would be 60 feet high.   146 _____

Then Borglum had workers dynamite the mountain in   154 _____

carefully selected places.   157 _____

The next task was to sculpt the faces out of the rough granite   170 _____

shapes created by the dynamite blasts. Borglum supervised miners   179 _____

who used drills, hammers, and chisels to shape and smooth the   190 _____

granite stone. Slowly the faces of the four presidents emerged.   200 _____

In 1941 the massive work of art was completed. The job had   212 _____

taken 14 years and had cost just under $1 million.   222 _____

Needs Work   1   2   3   4   5   Excellent
Paid attention to punctuation

Needs Work   1   2   3   4   5   Excellent
Sounded good

Total Words Read _____

Total Errors − _____

Correct WPM _____

18
Fiction

from *Gone-Away Lake*
by Elizabeth Enright

First Reading

	Words Read	Miscues

Aunt Hilda was Portia's third favorite woman in the world. — 10 _____

First came her mother, naturally, and after that Miss Hempel, — 20 _____

her English teacher, and after that came Aunt Hilda; but she was — 32 _____

so close behind Miss Hempel that it was more of a tie, really. — 45 _____

"Now, before we even show you the house, we must introduce — 56 _____

you to Katy's children," Aunt Hilda said, and she led them around — 68 _____

the house to a cellar door and down the steps to a big, clean — 82 _____

basement. And there in an old baby-pen were the puppies. — 92 _____

They had little dark flat faces like pansies, and ears that felt — 104 _____

like pieces of silk, and claws like the tips of knitting needles. Portia — 117 _____

had to pick one up first thing. It had a round little stomach and — 131 _____

wrinkled paws, and it nipped her finger gently and growled an — 142 _____

imitation growl. — 144 _____

"Any ideas for names yet? Any inspirations?" said Uncle Jake. — 154 _____

"I'll have to watch them for a while till I learn their characters," — 167 _____

Portia said rather importantly. She knew she was supposed to be — 178 _____

quite good at naming things. — 183 _____

Katy, who had followed them down, jumped over her own low — 194 _____

place in the railing and counted the puppies with her nose to see — 207 _____

that no one was missing. — 212 _____

Needs Work   1   2   3   4   5   Excellent
Paid attention to punctuation

Needs Work   1   2   3   4   5   Excellent
Sounded good

Total Words Read _____

Total Errors − _____

Correct WPM _____

from *Gone-Away Lake*
by Elizabeth Enright

Aunt Hilda was Portia's third favorite woman in the world.	10	_____
First came her mother, naturally, and after that Miss Hempel,	20	_____
her English teacher, and after that came Aunt Hilda; but she was	32	_____
so close behind Miss Hempel that it was more of a tie, really.	45	_____
"Now, before we even show you the house, we must introduce	56	_____
you to Katy's children," Aunt Hilda said, and she led them around	68	_____
the house to a cellar door and down the steps to a big, clean	82	_____
basement. And there in an old baby-pen were the puppies.	92	_____
They had little dark flat faces like pansies, and ears that felt	104	_____
like pieces of silk, and claws like the tips of knitting needles. Portia	117	_____
had to pick one up first thing. It had a round little stomach and	131	_____
wrinkled paws, and it nipped her finger gently and growled an	142	_____
imitation growl.	144	_____
"Any ideas for names yet? Any inspirations?" said Uncle Jake.	154	_____
"I'll have to watch them for a while till I learn their characters,"	167	_____
Portia said rather importantly. She knew she was supposed to be	178	_____
quite good at naming things.	183	_____
Katy, who had followed them down, jumped over her own low	194	_____
place in the railing and counted the puppies with her nose to see	207	_____
that no one was missing.	212	_____

Needs Work   1 2 3 4 5   Excellent
Paid attention to punctuation

Needs Work   1 2 3 4 5   Excellent
Sounded good

Total Words Read   _____

Total Errors   − _____

Correct WPM   _____

19 What Is Art?

Fiction

	Words Read	Miscues

☍☍☍

	Words Read	Miscues
Natasha spent several weeks working on an oil painting.	9	_____
She applied layers of color and then waited for the paint to dry	22	_____
before adding more layers of color. Under her brush, a peaceful	33	_____
woodland scene slowly took shape. Finally she put the last	43	_____
touches of paint on the canvas and set down her brush.	54	_____
While Natasha was putting the finishing touches on her	63	_____
painting, her brother Andrew sat in front of a computer screen.	74	_____
Using his computer's painting tools, he chose line widths and	84	_____
brush strokes. He selected colors and shades. With movements	93	_____
and clicks of Andrew's mouse, a stormy ocean scene quickly grew.	104	_____
With a tap of his finger, Andrew sent the image to his printer.	117	_____
"What do you think, Mom?" Natasha proudly presented	125	_____
her painting to her mother.	130	_____
"How about my artwork, Mom?" Andrew held up the	139	_____
color printout of his creation.	144	_____
"My painting took weeks!" said Natasha. "His took just	153	_____
a couple of hours. You can't call that art!"	162	_____
"I think you're both terrific artists," their mother said	171	_____
diplomatically. "It doesn't matter how long it took or what	181	_____
tools you used. You've both expressed your emotions and	190	_____
your ideas in your work, and that's what makes it art."	201	_____

Needs Work   1   2   3   4   5   Excellent
Paid attention to punctuation

Needs Work   1   2   3   4   5   Excellent
Sounded good

Total Words Read _____

Total Errors – _____

Correct WPM _____

19 What Is Art?

Fiction

	Words Read	Miscues

Natasha spent several weeks working on an oil painting. — 9 _____

She applied layers of color and then waited for the paint to dry — 22 _____

before adding more layers of color. Under her brush, a peaceful — 33 _____

woodland scene slowly took shape. Finally she put the last — 43 _____

touches of paint on the canvas and set down her brush. — 54 _____

While Natasha was putting the finishing touches on her — 63 _____

painting, her brother Andrew sat in front of a computer screen. — 74 _____

Using his computer's painting tools, he chose line widths and — 84 _____

brush strokes. He selected colors and shades. With movements — 93 _____

and clicks of Andrew's mouse, a stormy ocean scene quickly grew. — 104 _____

With a tap of his finger, Andrew sent the image to his printer. — 117 _____

"What do you think, Mom?" Natasha proudly presented — 125 _____

her painting to her mother. — 130 _____

"How about my artwork, Mom?" Andrew held up the — 139 _____

color printout of his creation. — 144 _____

"My painting took weeks!" said Natasha. "His took just — 153 _____

a couple of hours. You can't call that art!" — 162 _____

"I think you're both terrific artists," their mother said — 171 _____

diplomatically. "It doesn't matter how long it took or what — 181 _____

tools you used. You've both expressed your emotions and — 190 _____

your ideas in your work, and that's what makes it art." — 201 _____

Needs Work   1 2 3 4 5   Excellent
Paid attention to punctuation

Needs Work   1 2 3 4 5   Excellent
Sounded good

Total Words Read _____

Total Errors − _____

Correct WPM _____

Smashing the Land Speed Record

20

Nonfiction

	Words Read	Miscues

Richard Noble sat at the wheel of the Thrust 2 looking across   12   _____

the flat sands of Nevada's Black Rock Desert. Within moments   22   _____

he would fire the Rolls-Royce jet engine that powered his bullet-   33   _____

shaped vehicle. Would today be the day he broke the land speed   44   _____

record of 622 miles per hour set by Gary Gabelich?   54   _____

Speeds had increased greatly since Karl Benz's motor car   63   _____

chugged along at 9 miles per hour in 1886. Between 1924   74   _____

and 1935, Sir Malcolm Campbell, a legend in the world of auto   86   _____

racing, had broken the land speed record nine times! In 1964   97   _____

Sir Malcolm's son Donald set a record of 403 miles per hour.   109   _____

Noble knew that record was still standing for wheel-driven cars.   119   _____

Only jet-propelled vehicles had gone faster. Noble took a few   129   _____

deep breaths and readied himself for the challenge.   137   _____

With a roar like a jet plane taking off, the Thrust 2 hurtled   150   _____

across the sand. Faster and faster it went until it was just a blur.   164   _____

Then parachutes blossomed from its tail. There was no way   174   _____

ordinary brakes could stop a vehicle going at that speed! The   185   _____

parachutes filled with air, dragging against the car's forward   194   _____

motion until it rolled to a stop. Cheers greeted Noble as he   206   _____

climbed out. He had set a new record of 633 miles per hour!   219   _____

Needs Work 1 2 3 4 5 Excellent
Paid attention to punctuation

Needs Work 1 2 3 4 5 Excellent
Sounded good

Total Words Read _____

Total Errors − _____

Correct WPM _____

20

Nonfiction

Smashing the Land Speed Record

Second Reading

	Words Read	Miscues

Richard Noble sat at the wheel of the Thrust 2 looking across | 12 | _____

the flat sands of Nevada's Black Rock Desert. Within moments | 22 | _____

he would fire the Rolls-Royce jet engine that powered his bullet- | 33 | _____

shaped vehicle. Would today be the day he broke the land speed | 44 | _____

record of 622 miles per hour set by Gary Gabelich? | 54 | _____

Speeds had increased greatly since Karl Benz's motor car | 63 | _____

chugged along at 9 miles per hour in 1886. Between 1924 | 74 | _____

and 1935, Sir Malcolm Campbell, a legend in the world of auto | 86 | _____

racing, had broken the land speed record nine times! In 1964 | 97 | _____

Sir Malcolm's son Donald set a record of 403 miles per hour. | 109 | _____

Noble knew that record was still standing for wheel-driven cars. | 119 | _____

Only jet-propelled vehicles had gone faster. Noble took a few | 129 | _____

deep breaths and readied himself for the challenge. | 137 | _____

With a roar like a jet plane taking off, the Thrust 2 hurtled | 150 | _____

across the sand. Faster and faster it went until it was just a blur. | 164 | _____

Then parachutes blossomed from its tail. There was no way | 174 | _____

ordinary brakes could stop a vehicle going at that speed! The | 185 | _____

parachutes filled with air, dragging against the car's forward | 194 | _____

motion until it rolled to a stop. Cheers greeted Noble as he | 206 | _____

climbed out. He had set a new record of 633 miles per hour! | 219 | _____

Needs Work   1 2 3 4 5   Excellent
Paid attention to punctuation

Needs Work   1 2 3 4 5   Excellent
Sounded good

Total Words Read _____

Total Errors − _____

Correct WPM _____

21

Nonfiction

from *Dust Tracks on a Road*
by Zora Neale Hurston

First Reading

	Words Read	Miscues

That is how it was that my eyes were not in the book, working | 14 | _____

out the paragraph which I knew would be mine by counting the | 26 | _____

children ahead of me. I was observing our visitors, who held a | 38 | _____

book between them, following the lesson. They had shiny hair, | 48 | _____

mostly brownish. One had a looping gold chain around her | 58 | _____

neck. The other one was dressed all over in black and white with | 71 | _____

a pretty finger ring on her left hand. But the thing that held my | 85 | _____

eyes were their fingers. They were long and thin, and very white, | 97 | _____

except up near the tips. There they were baby pink. I had never | 110 | _____

seen such hands. It was a fascinating discovery for me. I wondered | 122 | _____

how they felt. I would have given those hands more attention, but | 134 | _____

the child before me was almost through. My turn next, so I got on | 148 | _____

my mark, bringing my eyes back to the book and made sure of my | 162 | _____

place. Some of the stories I had re-read several times, and this | 174 | _____

Greco-Roman myth was one of my favorites. I was exalted by it, | 186 | _____

and that is the way I read my paragraph. | 195 | _____

Needs Work   1   2   3   4   5   Excellent
Paid attention to punctuation

Needs Work   1   2   3   4   5   Excellent
Sounded good

Total Words Read _____

Total Errors − _____

Correct WPM _____

21

Nonfiction

from *Dust Tracks on a Road*

by Zora Neale Hurston

	Words Read	Miscues

That is how it was that my eyes were not in the book, working | 14 | _____
out the paragraph which I knew would be mine by counting the | 26 | _____
children ahead of me. I was observing our visitors, who held a | 38 | _____
book between them, following the lesson. They had shiny hair, | 48 | _____
mostly brownish. One had a looping gold chain around her | 58 | _____
neck. The other one was dressed all over in black and white with | 71 | _____
a pretty finger ring on her left hand. But the thing that held my | 85 | _____
eyes were their fingers. They were long and thin, and very white, | 97 | _____
except up near the tips. There they were baby pink. I had never | 110 | _____
seen such hands. It was a fascinating discovery for me. I wondered | 122 | _____
how they felt. I would have given those hands more attention, but | 134 | _____
the child before me was almost through. My turn next, so I got on | 148 | _____
my mark, bringing my eyes back to the book and made sure of my | 162 | _____
place. Some of the stories I had re-read several times, and this | 174 | _____
Greco–Roman myth was one of my favorites. I was exalted by it, | 186 | _____
and that is the way I read my paragraph. | 195 | _____

Needs Work   1   2   3   4   5   Excellent
Paid attention to punctuation

Needs Work   1   2   3   4   5   Excellent
Sounded good

Total Words Read _____

Total Errors − _____

Correct WPM _____

22
Nonfiction

from *Making Headlines:*
A Biography of Nellie Bly
by Kathy Lynn Emerson

First Reading

	Words Read	Miscues

~~~~~~~

	Words Read	Miscues
[Newswoman Nellie Bly] wanted to take another look at the	10	_____
factories. This time she went undercover, dressing herself as a	20	_____
poor woman looking for a job. She was hired at the first factory	33	_____
where she applied, though she had no skills. Her job was to hitch	46	_____
cables together in an assembly line with other young women.	56	_____
They could be fined for talking, or even for smiling, but Nellie did	69	_____
manage to learn that they all suffered from headaches.	78	_____
She soon understood why. The light was so dim that her head	90	_____
began to ache, too. Then her feet started to hurt, because she had	103	_____
to stand. Her hands became raw and started to bleed. Before long,	115	_____
she ached all over. Just like the workers in the bottle factory [that	128	_____
she had reported on earlier], these young women kept working in	139	_____
spite of their fear of blindness and the constant discomfort. They	150	_____
had to work to live.	155	_____
The women's supervisor kept urging them to work faster and	165	_____
faster. He paced back and forth behind them, yelling out threats	176	_____
and foul language. Since Nellie had been brought up to have	187	_____
good manners, she found it difficult to listen to curses and insults	199	_____
for hours on end. Finally, Nellie simply walked away from the	210	_____
assembly line to get a drink of water. The foreman fired her.	222	_____

Needs Work   1   2   3   4   5   Excellent
Paid attention to punctuation

Needs Work   1   2   3   4   5   Excellent
Sounded good

Total Words Read _____

Total Errors − _____

Correct WPM _____

22 Nonfiction

from *Making Headlines:*
A Biography of Nellie Bly
by Kathy Lynn Emerson

	Words Read	Miscues

[Newswoman Nellie Bly] wanted to take another look at the   10 _____
factories. This time she went undercover, dressing herself as a   20 _____
poor woman looking for a job. She was hired at the first factory   33 _____
where she applied, though she had no skills. Her job was to hitch   46 _____
cables together in an assembly line with other young women.   56 _____
They could be fined for talking, or even for smiling, but Nellie did   69 _____
manage to learn that they all suffered from headaches.   78 _____

She soon understood why. The light was so dim that her head   90 _____
began to ache, too. Then her feet started to hurt, because she had   103 _____
to stand. Her hands became raw and started to bleed. Before long,   115 _____
she ached all over. Just like the workers in the bottle factory [that   128 _____
she had reported on earlier], these young women kept working in   139 _____
spite of their fear of blindness and the constant discomfort. They   150 _____
had to work to live.   155 _____

The women's supervisor kept urging them to work faster and   165 _____
faster. He paced back and forth behind them, yelling out threats   176 _____
and foul language. Since Nellie had been brought up to have   187 _____
good manners, she found it difficult to listen to curses and insults   199 _____
for hours on end. Finally, Nellie simply walked away from the   210 _____
assembly line to get a drink of water. The foreman fired her.   222 _____

Needs Work   1   2   3   4   5   Excellent
Paid attention to punctuation

Needs Work   1   2   3   4   5   Excellent
Sounded good

Total Words Read _____

Total Errors − _____

Correct WPM _____

23

Fiction

from "The Stone and the Cross"
by Ciro Alegría
translated by Zoila Nelken and Rosalie Torres-Rioseco

First Reading

	Words Read	Miscues

Violent or calm, the wind did not stop blowing. Its persistence   11 _____
made it feel like an ice-cold bath. The boy's hands were stiff, and   24 _____
he felt that his legs were going to sleep. This might also be due   38 _____
to fatigue, and the altitude. Perhaps his blood was not circulating   49 _____
well. A slight humming had begun to sound in the depths of   61 _____
his ears. Making a swift decision, the boy dismounted, saying   71 _____
to his guide: 74 _____

"Pull my horse . . . Go on!"   79 _____

Without another word they began to walk, the guide and the   90 _____
two horses in front. The boy slung his poncho over his back. He   103 _____
felt the tips of his toes stiff and cold, and his legs obeyed him   117 _____
badly. He could hardly breathe, as if he needed much more rarefied   129 _____
air, and his heart was pounding. After walking along for ten minutes,   141 _____
he became very tired, but in spite of everything, he stubbornly   152 _____
continued to walk. He had heard his father say that in the Andes,   165 _____
one must sometimes travel at altitudes of ten, twelve, fourteen   175 _____
thousand feet, and even higher. He did not know at what altitude   187 _____
he found himself at that moment, but undoubtedly, it must be   198 _____
very high.   200 _____

Needs Work   1 2 3 4 5   Excellent
Paid attention to punctuation

Needs Work   1 2 3 4 5   Excellent
Sounded good

Total Words Read _____

Total Errors − _____

Correct WPM _____

23
Fiction

from "The Stone and the Cross"
by Ciro Alegría
translated by Zoila Nelken and Rosalie Torres-Rioseco

	Words Read	Miscues

Violent or calm, the wind did not stop blowing. Its persistence | 11 | _____
made it feel like an ice-cold bath. The boy's hands were stiff, and | 24 | _____
he felt that his legs were going to sleep. This might also be due | 38 | _____
to fatigue, and the altitude. Perhaps his blood was not circulating | 49 | _____
well. A slight humming had begun to sound in the depths of | 61 | _____
his ears. Making a swift decision, the boy dismounted, saying | 71 | _____
to his guide: | 74 | _____

"Pull my horse . . . Go on!" | 79 | _____

Without another word they began to walk, the guide and the | 90 | _____
two horses in front. The boy slung his poncho over his back. He | 103 | _____
felt the tips of his toes stiff and cold, and his legs obeyed him | 117 | _____
badly. He could hardly breathe, as if he needed much more rarefied | 129 | _____
air, and his heart was pounding. After walking along for ten minutes, | 141 | _____
he became very tired, but in spite of everything, he stubbornly | 152 | _____
continued to walk. He had heard his father say that in the Andes, | 165 | _____
one must sometimes travel at altitudes of ten, twelve, fourteen | 175 | _____
thousand feet, and even higher. He did not know at what altitude | 187 | _____
he found himself at that moment, but undoubtedly, it must be | 198 | _____
very high. | 200 | _____

Needs Work   1   2   3   4   5   Excellent
Paid attention to punctuation

Needs Work   1   2   3   4   5   Excellent
Sounded good

Total Words Read _____

Total Errors − _____

Correct WPM _____

24
Fiction

from "Through the Tunnel"
by Doris Lessing

	Words Read	Miscues
[Jerry] came to the surface, swam to shore, and went back to	12	_____
the villa to wait for his mother. Soon she walked slowly up the	25	_____
path, swinging her striped bag, the flushed, naked arm dangling	35	_____
beside her. "I want some swimming goggles," he panted, defiant	45	_____
and beseeching.	47	_____
She gave him a patient, inquisitive look as she said casually,	58	_____
"Well, of course, darling."	62	_____
But now, now, now! He must have them this minute, and no	74	_____
other time. He nagged and pestered until she went with him to	86	_____
a shop. As soon as she had bought the goggles, he grabbed them	99	_____
from her hand as if she were going to claim them for herself, and	113	_____
was off, running down the steep path to the bay.	123	_____
Jerry swam out to the big barrier rock, adjusted the goggles,	134	_____
and dived. The impact of the water broke the rubber-enclosed	144	_____
vacuum, and the goggles came loose. He understood that he must	155	_____
swim down to the base of the rock from the surface of the water.	169	_____
He fixed the goggles tight and firm, filled his lungs, and floated,	181	_____
face down, on the water. Now, he could see. It was as if he had	196	_____
eyes of a different kind—fish eyes that showed everything clear	207	_____
and delicate and wavering in the bright water.	215	_____

Needs Work   1   2   3   4   5   Excellent
Paid attention to punctuation

Needs Work   1   2   3   4   5   Excellent
Sounded good

Total Words Read _____

Total Errors − _____

Correct WPM _____

24

Fiction

from "Through the Tunnel"

by Doris Lessing

	Words Read	Miscues
[Jerry] came to the surface, swam to shore, and went back to	12	_____
the villa to wait for his mother. Soon she walked slowly up the	25	_____
path, swinging her striped bag, the flushed, naked arm dangling	35	_____
beside her. "I want some swimming goggles," he panted, defiant	45	_____
and beseeching.	47	_____
She gave him a patient, inquisitive look as she said casually,	58	_____
"Well, of course, darling."	62	_____
But now, now, now! He must have them this minute, and no	74	_____
other time. He nagged and pestered until she went with him to	86	_____
a shop. As soon as she had bought the goggles, he grabbed them	99	_____
from her hand as if she were going to claim them for herself, and	113	_____
was off, running down the steep path to the bay.	123	_____
Jerry swam out to the big barrier rock, adjusted the goggles,	134	_____
and dived. The impact of the water broke the rubber-enclosed	144	_____
vacuum, and the goggles came loose. He understood that he must	155	_____
swim down to the base of the rock from the surface of the water.	169	_____
He fixed the goggles tight and firm, filled his lungs, and floated,	181	_____
face down, on the water. Now, he could see. It was as if he had	196	_____
eyes of a different kind—fish eyes that showed everything clear	207	_____
and delicate and wavering in the bright water.	215	_____

Needs Work   1   2   3   4   5   Excellent
Paid attention to punctuation

Needs Work   1   2   3   4   5   Excellent
Sounded good

Total Words Read _____

Total Errors − _____

Correct WPM _____

25
Fiction

from "Rules of the Game"
by Amy Tan

First Reading

	Words Read	Miscues

On a cold spring afternoon, while walking home from school, **10** _____

I detoured through the playground at the end of our alley. I saw a **24** _____

group of old men, two seated across a folding table playing a **36** _____

game of chess, others smoking pipes, eating peanuts, and **45** _____

watching. I ran home and grabbed Vincent's chess set, which was **56** _____

bound in a cardboard box with rubber bands. I also carefully **67** _____

selected two prized rolls of Life Savers. I came back to the park **80** _____

and approached a man who was observing the game. **89** _____

"Want to play?" I asked him. His face widened with surprise **100** _____

and he grinned as he looked at the box under my arm. **112** _____

"Little sister, been a long time since I play with dolls," he said, **125** _____

smiling benevolently. I quickly put the box down next to him on **137** _____

the bench and displayed my retort. **143** _____

Lau Po, as he allowed me to call him, turned out to be a much **158** _____

better player than my brothers. I lost many games and many Life **170** _____

Savers. But over the weeks, with each diminishing roll of candies, **181** _____

I added new secrets. Lau Po gave me the names. The double **193** _____

Attack from the East and West Shores. Throwing Stones on the **204** _____

Drowning Man. The Sudden Meeting of the Clan. **212** _____

Needs Work   1 2 3 4 5   Excellent
Paid attention to punctuation

Needs Work   1 2 3 4 5   Excellent
Sounded good

Total Words Read _____

Total Errors − _____

Correct WPM _____

25 Fiction

from "Rules of the Game"
by Amy Tan

	Words Read	Miscues

On a cold spring afternoon, while walking home from school,   10 _____

I detoured through the playground at the end of our alley. I saw a   24 _____

group of old men, two seated across a folding table playing a   36 _____

game of chess, others smoking pipes, eating peanuts, and   45 _____

watching. I ran home and grabbed Vincent's chess set, which was   56 _____

bound in a cardboard box with rubber bands. I also carefully   67 _____

selected two prized rolls of Life Savers. I came back to the park   80 _____

and approached a man who was observing the game.   89 _____

"Want to play?" I asked him. His face widened with surprise   100 _____

and he grinned as he looked at the box under my arm.   112 _____

"Little sister, been a long time since I play with dolls," he said,   125 _____

smiling benevolently. I quickly put the box down next to him on   137 _____

the bench and displayed my retort.   143 _____

Lau Po, as he allowed me to call him, turned out to be a much   158 _____

better player than my brothers. I lost many games and many Life   170 _____

Savers. But over the weeks, with each diminishing roll of candies,   181 _____

I added new secrets. Lau Po gave me the names. The double   193 _____

Attack from the East and West Shores. Throwing Stones on the   204 _____

Drowning Man. The Sudden Meeting of the Clan.   212 _____

Needs Work 1 2 3 4 5 Excellent
Paid attention to punctuation

Needs Work 1 2 3 4 5 Excellent
Sounded good

Total Words Read _____

Total Errors − _____

Correct WPM _____

26
Fiction

from *Le Morte d'Arthur*
by Sir Thomas Malory
retold by Keith Baines

	Words Read	Miscues

Arthur found the door of the lodging locked and bolted,   10 _____

the landlord and his wife having left for the tournament. In   21 _____

order not to disappoint his brother, he rode on to St. Paul's,   33 _____

determined to get for him the sword which was lodged in the   45 _____

stone. The yard was empty, the guard also having slipped off   56 _____

to see the tournament, so Arthur strode up to the sword, and,   68 _____

without troubling to read the inscription, tugged it free. He   78 _____

then rode straight back to Sir Kay and presented him with it.   90 _____

Sir Kay recognized the sword, and taking it to Sir Ector, said,   102 _____

"Father, the succession falls to me, for I have here the sword that   115 _____

was lodged in the stone." But Sir Ector insisted that they should   127 _____

all ride to the churchyard, and once there bound Sir Kay by oath   140 _____

to tell how he had come by the sword. Sir Kay then admitted that   154 _____

Arthur had given it to him. Sir Ector turned to Arthur and said,   167 _____

"Was the sword not guarded?"   172 _____

"It was not," Arthur replied.   177 _____

"Would you please thrust it into the stone again?" said Sir   188 _____

Ector. Arthur did so, and first Sir Ector and then Sir Kay tried to   202 _____

remove it, but both were unable to. Then Arthur, for the second   214 _____

time, pulled it out.   218 _____

Needs Work   1   2   3   4   5   Excellent
    Paid attention to punctuation

Needs Work   1   2   3   4   5   Excellent
    Sounded good

Total Words Read   _____

Total Errors   − _____

Correct WPM   _____

26

Fiction

from *Le Morte d'Arthur*
by Sir Thomas Malory
retold by Keith Baines

	Words Read	Miscues

Arthur found the door of the lodging locked and bolted, · 10 · _____

the landlord and his wife having left for the tournament. In · 21 · _____

order not to disappoint his brother, he rode on to St. Paul's, · 33 · _____

determined to get for him the sword which was lodged in the · 45 · _____

stone. The yard was empty, the guard also having slipped off · 56 · _____

to see the tournament, so Arthur strode up to the sword, and, · 68 · _____

without troubling to read the inscription, tugged it free. He · 78 · _____

then rode straight back to Sir Kay and presented him with it. · 90 · _____

Sir Kay recognized the sword, and taking it to Sir Ector, said, · 102 · _____

"Father, the succession falls to me, for I have here the sword that · 115 · _____

was lodged in the stone." But Sir Ector insisted that they should · 127 · _____

all ride to the churchyard, and once there bound Sir Kay by oath · 140 · _____

to tell how he had come by the sword. Sir Kay then admitted that · 154 · _____

Arthur had given it to him. Sir Ector turned to Arthur and said, · 167 · _____

"Was the sword not guarded?" · 172 · _____

"It was not," Arthur replied. · 177 · _____

"Would you please thrust it into the stone again?" said Sir · 188 · _____

Ector. Arthur did so, and first Sir Ector and then Sir Kay tried to · 202 · _____

remove it, but both were unable to. Then Arthur, for the second · 214 · _____

time, pulled it out. · 218 · _____

Needs Work   1   2   3   4   5   Excellent
Paid attention to punctuation

Needs Work   1   2   3   4   5   Excellent
Sounded good

Total Words Read _____

Total Errors   − _____

Correct WPM _____

27

Nonfiction

from *Hiding to Survive*
by Maxine B. Rosenberg

First Reading

	Words Read	Miscues

By now the Germans were everywhere. It got so dangerous,   10 _____
we could no longer live upstairs and instead moved into the cellar   22 _____
under the kitchen. But Herman thought that wasn't safe either   32 _____
and decided we should build a bunker next to the cellar, where   44 _____
the Germans were less likely to look. He and Mr. Karashka   55 _____
designed the room.   58 _____

It was seven feet long and very narrow. To get in and out,   71 _____
they made a trap door that opened into the hallway. It had   83 _____
wooden planks on top that matched the flooring. Underneath   92 _____
it was insulated with blankets and cotton so it wouldn't sound   103 _____
hollow when someone walked on it.   109 _____

For one week we all helped build the bunker, sleeping in   120 _____
the day and digging at night. Hour after hour we shoveled earth   132 _____
into bags which Mr. Karashka emptied onto his field. Finally   142 _____
the bunker was finished. It was tiny, dark, and uncomfortable.   152 _____
Although we each had a quilt and a wooden board to sleep on,   165 _____
the earthen floor was always damp, so our clothing and blankets   176 _____
smelled musty.   178 _____

Because there was hardly any fresh air in the bunker, we kept   190 _____
the trap door braced open with a forked stick. At night the adults   203 _____
took turns being on guard to alert us if there was trouble.   215 _____

Needs Work   1   2   3   4   5   Excellent
Paid attention to punctuation

Needs Work   1   2   3   4   5   Excellent
Sounded good

Total Words Read   _____

Total Errors   − _____

Correct WPM   _____

from *Hiding to Survive*

by Maxine B. Rosenberg

	Words Read	Miscues
By now the Germans were everywhere. It got so dangerous,	10	_____
we could no longer live upstairs and instead moved into the cellar	22	_____
under the kitchen. But Herman thought that wasn't safe either	32	_____
and decided we should build a bunker next to the cellar, where	44	_____
the Germans were less likely to look. He and Mr. Karashka	55	_____
designed the room.	58	_____
It was seven feet long and very narrow. To get in and out,	71	_____
they made a trap door that opened into the hallway. It had	83	_____
wooden planks on top that matched the flooring. Underneath	92	_____
it was insulated with blankets and cotton so it wouldn't sound	103	_____
hollow when someone walked on it.	109	_____
For one week we all helped build the bunker, sleeping in	120	_____
the day and digging at night. Hour after hour we shoveled earth	132	_____
into bags which Mr. Karashka emptied onto his field. Finally	142	_____
the bunker was finished. It was tiny, dark, and uncomfortable.	152	_____
Although we each had a quilt and a wooden board to sleep on,	165	_____
the earthen floor was always damp, so our clothing and blankets	176	_____
smelled musty.	178	_____
Because there was hardly any fresh air in the bunker, we kept	190	_____
the trap door braced open with a forked stick. At night the adults	203	_____
took turns being on guard to alert us if there was trouble.	215	_____

Needs Work   1   2   3   4   5   Excellent
Paid attention to punctuation

Needs Work   1   2   3   4   5   Excellent
Sounded good

Total Words Read _____

Total Errors − _____

Correct WPM _____

Winston Churchill's School Days

28 Nonfiction

	Words Read	Miscues

Like most boys of his time from wealthy families, Winston | 10 | _____

Churchill was sent to boarding school at the age of seven. | 21 | _____

His parents deposited him, already homesick and thoroughly | 29 | _____

miserable, at the school one dark November evening. | 37 | _____

Having missed part of the term, Winston had to catch up. | 48 | _____

He was taken to the Latin teacher, who gave him a paper with | 61 | _____

six forms of the Latin noun *mensa* to memorize. The words had | 73 | _____

no meaning for him, but Winston memorized them anyway. The | 83 | _____

teacher came back and was pleased that Winston could recite the | 94 | _____

forms of the noun perfectly. | 99 | _____

Then Winston made his first big mistake. "What does it | 109 | _____

mean?" he asked. The teacher explained that *mensa* meant "table." | 119 | _____

But why, Winston wanted to know, did it also mean "O table"? | 131 | _____

Somewhat impatiently, the teacher explained that this was the | 140 | _____

form of the word one used when one wanted to speak to a table. | 154 | _____

"But I never do!" Churchill responded. | 160 | _____

Annoyed, the teacher told him that such impertinence would | 169 | _____

be punished severely. So in his first hours at school, Churchill had | 181 | _____

already begun to gain a reputation for being both too smart for | 193 | _____

his own good and too stubborn to learn. | 201 | _____

Needs Work   1   2   3   4   5   Excellent
Paid attention to punctuation

Needs Work   1   2   3   4   5   Excellent
Sounded good

Total Words Read _____

Total Errors – _____

Correct WPM _____

28 Winston Churchill's School Days

Nonfiction

	Words Read	Miscues

Like most boys of his time from wealthy families, Winston Churchill was sent to boarding school at the age of seven. His parents deposited him, already homesick and thoroughly miserable, at the school one dark November evening.

Having missed part of the term, Winston had to catch up. He was taken to the Latin teacher, who gave him a paper with six forms of the Latin noun *mensa* to memorize. The words had no meaning for him, but Winston memorized them anyway. The teacher came back and was pleased that Winston could recite the forms of the noun perfectly.

Then Winston made his first big mistake. "What does it mean?" he asked. The teacher explained that *mensa* meant "table." But why, Winston wanted to know, did it also mean "O table"? Somewhat impatiently, the teacher explained that this was the form of the word one used when one wanted to speak to a table.

"But I never do!" Churchill responded.

Annoyed, the teacher told him that such impertinence would be punished severely. So in his first hours at school, Churchill had already begun to gain a reputation for being both too smart for his own good and too stubborn to learn.

Words Read
10
21
29
37
48
61
73
83
94
99
109
119
131
140
154
160
169
181
193
201

Needs Work   1 2 3 4 5   Excellent
Paid attention to punctuation

Needs Work   1 2 3 4 5   Excellent
Sounded good

Total Words Read _____

Total Errors − _____

Correct WPM _____

29

Fiction

from "Neighbor Rosicky"
by Willa Cather

First Reading

	Words Read	Miscues

The cramp began in his chest, like yesterday. [Rosicky] put — 10 — _____
his pipe cautiously down on the windowsill and bent over to ease — 22 — _____
the pull. No use,—he had better try to get to his bed if he could. — 38 — _____
He rose and groped his way across the familiar floor, which was — 50 — _____
rising and falling like the deck of a ship. At the door he fell. — 64 — _____
When [his wife] Mary came in, she found him lying there, — 75 — _____
and the moment she touched him she knew that he was gone. — 87 — _____

    Doctor Ed was away when Rosicky died, and for the first few — 99 — _____
weeks after he got home he was hard driven. Every day he said — 112 — _____
to himself that he must get out to see that family that had lost — 126 — _____
their father. One soft, warm moonlight night in early summer he — 137 — _____
started for the farm. His mind was on other things, and not until — 150 — _____
his road ran by the graveyard did he realize that Rosicky wasn't — 162 — _____
[at his house] over there on the hill, where the red lamplight — 174 — _____
shone, but here, in the moonlight. He stopped his car, shut off — 186 — _____
the engine, and sat there for a while. — 194 — _____

    A sudden hush had fallen on his soul. Everything here seemed — 205 — _____
strangely moving and significant, though signifying what, he did — 214 — _____
not know. — 216 — _____

Needs Work 1 2 3 4 5 Excellent
Paid attention to punctuation

Needs Work 1 2 3 4 5 Excellent
Sounded good

Total Words Read _____

Total Errors − _____

Correct WPM _____

from "Neighbor Rosicky"
by Willa Cather

The cramp began in his chest, like yesterday. [Rosicky] put	10	_____
his pipe cautiously down on the windowsill and bent over to ease	22	_____
the pull. No use,—he had better try to get to his bed if he could.	38	_____
He rose and groped his way across the familiar floor, which was	50	_____
rising and falling like the deck of a ship. At the door he fell.	64	_____
When [his wife] Mary came in, she found him lying there,	75	_____
and the moment she touched him she knew that he was gone.	87	_____
Doctor Ed was away when Rosicky died, and for the first few	99	_____
weeks after he got home he was hard driven. Every day he said	112	_____
to himself that he must get out to see that family that had lost	126	_____
their father. One soft, warm moonlight night in early summer he	137	_____
started for the farm. His mind was on other things, and not until	150	_____
his road ran by the graveyard did he realize that Rosicky wasn't	162	_____
[at his house] over there on the hill, where the red lamplight	174	_____
shone, but here, in the moonlight. He stopped his car, shut off	186	_____
the engine, and sat there for a while.	194	_____
A sudden hush had fallen on his soul. Everything here seemed	205	_____
strangely moving and significant, though signifying what, he did	214	_____
not know.	216	_____

Needs Work   1 2 3 4 5   Excellent
Paid attention to punctuation

Needs Work   1 2 3 4 5   Excellent
Sounded good

Total Words Read _____

Total Errors − _____

Correct WPM _____

58

30

Fiction

from "The Old Demon"
by Pearl S. Buck

	Words Read	Miscues

Old Mrs. Wang knew, of course, that there was a war.   11   _____

Everybody had known for a long time that there was a war   23   _____

going on and that Japanese were killing Chinese. But still it was   35   _____

not real and no more than hearsay since none of the Wangs   47   _____

had been killed. The Village of Three Mile Wangs on the flat   59   _____

banks of the Yellow River, which was old Mrs. Wang's clan village,   71   _____

had never seen a Japanese. This was how they came to be talking   84   _____

about Japanese at all.   88   _____

It was evening and early summer, and after her supper Mrs.   99   _____

Wang had climbed the dike steps, as she did every day, to see how   113   _____

high the river had risen. She was much more afraid of the river   126   _____

than of the Japanese. She knew what the river would do. And one   139   _____

by one the villagers had followed her up the dike, and now they   152   _____

stood staring down at the malicious yellow water, curling along   162   _____

like a lot of snakes, and biting at the high dike banks.   174   _____

"I never saw it as high as this so early," Mrs. Wang said. She   188   _____

sat down on a bamboo stool that her grandson, Little Pig, had   200   _____

brought for her, and spat into the water.   208   _____

Needs Work   1   2   3   4   5   Excellent
Paid attention to punctuation

Needs Work   1   2   3   4   5   Excellent
Sounded good

Total Words Read   _____

Total Errors − _____

Correct WPM   _____

30

Fiction

from "The Old Demon"
by Pearl S. Buck

	Words Read	Miscues
Old Mrs. Wang knew, of course, that there was a war.	11	_____
Everybody had known for a long time that there was a war	23	_____
going on and that Japanese were killing Chinese. But still it was	35	_____
not real and no more than hearsay since none of the Wangs	47	_____
had been killed. The Village of Three Mile Wangs on the flat	59	_____
banks of the Yellow River, which was old Mrs. Wang's clan village,	71	_____
had never seen a Japanese. This was how they came to be talking	84	_____
about Japanese at all.	88	_____
It was evening and early summer, and after her supper Mrs.	99	_____
Wang had climbed the dike steps, as she did every day, to see how	113	_____
high the river had risen. She was much more afraid of the river	126	_____
than of the Japanese. She knew what the river would do. And one	139	_____
by one the villagers had followed her up the dike, and now they	152	_____
stood staring down at the malicious yellow water, curling along	162	_____
like a lot of snakes, and biting at the high dike banks.	174	_____
"I never saw it as high as this so early," Mrs. Wang said. She	188	_____
sat down on a bamboo stool that her grandson, Little Pig, had	200	_____
brought for her, and spat into the water.	208	_____

Needs Work   1 2 3 4 5   Excellent
Paid attention to punctuation

Needs Work   1 2 3 4 5   Excellent
Sounded good

Total Words Read _____

Total Errors − _____

Correct WPM _____

31

Nonfiction

from *Rosa Parks: My Story*
by Rosa Parks
with Jim Haskins

First Reading

	Words Read	Miscues

Most black people had finally had enough of segregation on the | 11 | _____

buses. They stayed off those buses. They waited at the bus stops | 23 | _____

for the black-owned cabs to come along. Or they walked or got a | 36 | _____

ride. As a result, the Montgomery city buses were practically | 46 | _____

empty. Oh, a few black people took the buses, but they were mostly | 59 | _____

people who had not heard about the protest. Some of them were | 71 | _____

scared away from the buses. The city police had vowed to protect | 83 | _____

anyone who wanted to ride, and each bus had two motorcycle | 94 | _____

escorts. But some of the people who didn't know what was going | 106 | _____

on thought the police were there to arrest them for riding the | 118 | _____

buses, not to protect them. And then there were those few who | 130 | _____

didn't want to be inconvenienced. When the bus they were on | 141 | _____

passed a bus stop full of black people waiting for cabs, they | 153 | _____

ducked down low so nobody would see them. | 161 | _____

That day I had no idea what the result was going to be, but | 175 | _____

I think everybody was quite amazed at that demonstration of | 185 | _____

people staying off the buses. It was a surprise to everybody, | 196 | _____

I think. As [NAACP activist] Mr. Nixon said, "We surprised | 206 | _____

ourselves." Never before had black people demonstrated so | 214 | _____

clearly how much those city buses depended on their business. | 224 | _____

Needs Work 1 2 3 4 5 Excellent
Paid attention to punctuation

Needs Work 1 2 3 4 5 Excellent
Sounded good

Total Words Read _____

Total Errors − _____

Correct WPM _____

from *Rosa Parks: My Story*
by Rosa Parks
with Jim Haskins

	Words Read	Miscues

Most black people had finally had enough of segregation on the | 11 | _____
buses. They stayed off those buses. They waited at the bus stops | 23 | _____
for the black-owned cabs to come along. Or they walked or got a | 36 | _____
ride. As a result, the Montgomery city buses were practically | 46 | _____
empty. Oh, a few black people took the buses, but they were mostly | 59 | _____
people who had not heard about the protest. Some of them were | 71 | _____
scared away from the buses. The city police had vowed to protect | 83 | _____
anyone who wanted to ride, and each bus had two motorcycle | 94 | _____
escorts. But some of the people who didn't know what was going | 106 | _____
on thought the police were there to arrest them for riding the | 118 | _____
buses, not to protect them. And then there were those few who | 130 | _____
didn't want to be inconvenienced. When the bus they were on | 141 | _____
passed a bus stop full of black people waiting for cabs, they | 153 | _____
ducked down low so nobody would see them. | 161 | _____

That day I had no idea what the result was going to be, but | 175 | _____
I think everybody was quite amazed at that demonstration of | 185 | _____
people staying off the buses. It was a surprise to everybody, | 196 | _____
I think. As [NAACP activist] Mr. Nixon said, "We surprised | 206 | _____
ourselves." Never before had black people demonstrated so | 214 | _____
clearly how much those city buses depended on their business. | 224 | _____

Needs Work   1   2   3   4   5   Excellent
Paid attention to punctuation

Needs Work   1   2   3   4   5   Excellent
Sounded good

Total Words Read   _____

Total Errors   − _____

Correct WPM   _____

32

Nonfiction

Working on the Road

First Reading

	Words Read	Miscues

        Maria Gonzales is a flagperson on a road crew repairing a | 11 | _____
state highway. She reports to work before 7:00 A.M. to ride with | 23 | _____
the crew to the work area. Maria goes immediately to her place; | 35 | _____
she must control traffic while the area is being set up. It is still | 49 | _____
chilly, but later it will be blistering hot. At least it's not raining. | 62 | _____
Her crew works in all conditions. | 68 | _____

        Today they close one lane of a two-lane highway around | 78 | _____
a curve. Maria isn't able to see her partner at the other end. | 91 | _____
She stays in contact by radio. Since traffic in both directions | 102 | _____
uses one lane, she must make sure the road is clear before starting | 115 | _____
oncoming traffic. She must be vigilant and make no mistakes. | 125 | _____

        Breaks are short. Standing all day is hard, but even when there | 137 | _____
is no traffic, she cannot sit down or relax. The job is too important. | 151 | _____

        At the end of the day, Maria is the last to leave. The road must | 166 | _____
be clear and the road cones stowed before both lanes are opened. | 178 | _____
She is tired, but she considers herself lucky, because it is a good | 191 | _____
job and she is well paid. | 197 | _____

Needs Work   1   2   3   4   5   Excellent
        Paid attention to punctuation

Needs Work   1   2   3   4   5   Excellent
        Sounded good

Total Words Read _____

Total Errors – _____

Correct WPM _____

Working on the Road

	Words Read	Miscues

Maria Gonzales is a flagperson on a road crew repairing a | 11 | _____
state highway. She reports to work before 7:00 A.M. to ride with | 23 | _____
the crew to the work area. Maria goes immediately to her place; | 35 | _____
she must control traffic while the area is being set up. It is still | 49 | _____
chilly, but later it will be blistering hot. At least it's not raining. | 62 | _____
Her crew works in all conditions. | 68 | _____

Today they close one lane of a two-lane highway around | 78 | _____
a curve. Maria isn't able to see her partner at the other end. | 91 | _____
She stays in contact by radio. Since traffic in both directions | 102 | _____
uses one lane, she must make sure the road is clear before starting | 115 | _____
oncoming traffic. She must be vigilant and make no mistakes. | 125 | _____

Breaks are short. Standing all day is hard, but even when there | 137 | _____
is no traffic, she cannot sit down or relax. The job is too important. | 151 | _____

At the end of the day, Maria is the last to leave. The road must | 166 | _____
be clear and the road cones stowed before both lanes are opened. | 178 | _____
She is tired, but she considers herself lucky, because it is a good | 191 | _____
job and she is well paid. | 197 | _____

Needs Work   1   2   3   4   5   Excellent
Paid attention to punctuation

Needs Work   1   2   3   4   5   Excellent
Sounded good

Total Words Read _____

Total Errors – _____

Correct WPM _____

Reader ______________________ Checker ______________________

33

Fiction

from *Banner in the Sky*

by James Ramsey Ullman

First Reading

Words Read | **Miscues**

While he slept, he dreamt *the dream.* The setting was the same 12 ____
as always: a thin ridge of rock, a dome of snow, and, beyond the 26 ____
dome, the blue and gleaming emptiness of the sky. But whereas, 37 ____
before, he had invariably been alone, there were now others with 48 ____
him. Captain Winter and his Uncle Franz, a few paces back, and 60 ____
behind them a small shadowy figure—perhaps his mother?—who 70 ____
seemed to be calling him. 75 ____

All the rest, though, was exactly as in the other dreams. He, 87 ____
Rudi, stepped up from the rock onto the snow. He stood on the 100 ____
very crest of the snow, and all the mountain, all Switzerland, all 112 ____
the world, was beneath him. For a moment he knelt. Then, rising, 124 ____
he unstrapped a pole he had been carrying on his back, took a red 138 ____
flannel shirt from his knapsack, and tied the shirt to the pole by 151 ____
its sleeves. He set the pole into the snow—the magical, shining 163 ____
snow upon which no man had ever stood before; and now a 175 ____
wind was blowing, and the shirt flapped like a flame on the white 188 ____
summit of the Citadel. 192 ____

Needs Work 1 2 3 4 5 Excellent
Paid attention to punctuation

Needs Work 1 2 3 4 5 Excellent
Sounded good

Total Words Read ________

Total Errors – ________

Correct WPM ________

33

Fiction

from *Banner in the Sky*

by James Ramsey Ullman

	Words Read	Miscues

While he slept, he dreamt *the dream*. The setting was the same as always: a thin ridge of rock, a dome of snow, and, beyond the dome, the blue and gleaming emptiness of the sky. But whereas, before, he had invariably been alone, there were now others with him. Captain Winter and his Uncle Franz, a few paces back, and behind them a small shadowy figure—perhaps his mother?—who seemed to be calling him.

All the rest, though, was exactly as in the other dreams. He, Rudi, stepped up from the rock onto the snow. He stood on the very crest of the snow, and all the mountain, all Switzerland, all the world, was beneath him. For a moment he knelt. Then, rising, he unstrapped a pole he had been carrying on his back, took a red flannel shirt from his knapsack, and tied the shirt to the pole by its sleeves. He set the pole into the snow—the magical, shining snow upon which no man had ever stood before; and now a wind was blowing, and the shirt flapped like a flame on the white summit of the Citadel.

Words Read
12
26
37
48
60
70
75
87
100
112
124
138
151
163
175
188
192

Needs Work   1 2 3 4 5   Excellent
Paid attention to punctuation

Needs Work   1 2 3 4 5   Excellent
Sounded good

Total Words Read _____

Total Errors − _____

Correct WPM _____

34
Fiction

from **"Another April"**
by Jesse Stuart

First Reading

	Words Read	Miscues

❦❦❦

	Words Read	Miscues
As I watched Grandpa go down the path toward the hog pen	12	_____
he stopped to examine every little thing along his path. Once he	24	_____
waved his cane at a butterfly as it zigzagged over his head, its	37	_____
polka-dot wings fanning the blue April air. Grandpa would stand	47	_____
when a puff of wind came along, and hold his face against the	60	_____
wind and let the wind play with his white whiskers. I thought	72	_____
maybe his face was hot under his beard and he was letting the	85	_____
wind cool his face. When he reached the hog pen he called the	98	_____
hogs down to the fence. They came running and grunting to	109	_____
Grandpa just like they were talking to him. I knew that Grandpa	121	_____
couldn't hear them trying to talk to him but he could see their	134	_____
mouths working and he knew they were trying to say something.	145	_____
He leaned his cane against the hog pen, reached over the fence,	157	_____
and patted the hogs' heads. Grandpa didn't miss patting one of	168	_____
our seven hogs.	171	_____
As he toddled up the little path alongside the hog pen he	183	_____
stopped under a blooming dogwood. He pulled a white blossom	193	_____
from a bough that swayed over the path above his head.	204	_____

Needs Work   1 2 3 4 5   Excellent
        Paid attention to punctuation

Needs Work   1 2 3 4 5   Excellent
        Sounded good

Total Words Read _____

Total Errors – _____

Correct WPM _____

34

Fiction

from "Another April"

by Jesse Stuart

	Words Read	Miscues

As I watched Grandpa go down the path toward the hog pen | 12 | _____

he stopped to examine every little thing along his path. Once he | 24 | _____

waved his cane at a butterfly as it zigzagged over his head, its | 37 | _____

polka-dot wings fanning the blue April air. Grandpa would stand | 47 | _____

when a puff of wind came along, and hold his face against the | 60 | _____

wind and let the wind play with his white whiskers. I thought | 72 | _____

maybe his face was hot under his beard and he was letting the | 85 | _____

wind cool his face. When he reached the hog pen he called the | 98 | _____

hogs down to the fence. They came running and grunting to | 109 | _____

Grandpa just like they were talking to him. I knew that Grandpa | 121 | _____

couldn't hear them trying to talk to him but he could see their | 134 | _____

mouths working and he knew they were trying to say something. | 145 | _____

He leaned his cane against the hog pen, reached over the fence, | 157 | _____

and patted the hogs' heads. Grandpa didn't miss patting one of | 168 | _____

our seven hogs. | 171 | _____

As he toddled up the little path alongside the hog pen he | 183 | _____

stopped under a blooming dogwood. He pulled a white blossom | 193 | _____

from a bough that swayed over the path above his head. | 204 | _____

Needs Work   1   2   3   4   5   Excellent
Paid attention to punctuation

Needs Work   1   2   3   4   5   Excellent
Sounded good

Total Words Read _____

Total Errors   – _____

Correct WPM _____

Father David's Deer

35

Nonfiction

First Reading

	Words Read	Miscues

In 1865 a French missionary to China named Father David   **10**   _____

saw large, handsome deer in the Royal Hunting Preserve of Beijing.   **21**   _____

His discovery proved to be a kind of deer hitherto unknown in   **33**   _____

Europe. The deer, already quite rare, had an ancient history in   **44**   _____

China. Legend said that they were harnessed to the chariots of   **55**   _____

Chinese gods.   **57**   _____

European zoos immediately wanted the deer, and China gave   **66**   _____

some away. Then in 1900 soldiers shot the remaining deer during   **77**   _____

a rebellion. There were no more Father David's deer in China.   **88**   _____

In England a British duke realized that European zoos had   **98**   _____

the only surviving Father David's deer. He bought them all—18   **109**   _____

of them—and set them loose on his estate. After he died, his son   **123**   _____

and then his grandson took over their care.   **131**   _____

In 1980 representatives of the Chinese government   **138**   _____

approached the duke's family in England. Might they have   **147**   _____

some of their native deer back? After much discussion, a plan   **158**   _____

was approved and a suitable place chosen. Chinese workers   **167**   _____

planted grass and built a high wall around the parkland where   **178**   _____

the deer would be released. In 1986, for the first time in 86   **191**   _____

years, 22 of China's native deer were back in China.   **201**   _____

Needs Work   1   2   3   4   5   Excellent
Paid attention to punctuation

Needs Work   1   2   3   4   5   Excellent
Sounded good

Total Words Read _____

Total Errors – _____

Correct WPM _____

Father David's Deer

	Words Read	Miscues
In 1865 a French missionary to China named Father David	10	_____
saw large, handsome deer in the Royal Hunting Preserve of Beijing.	21	_____
His discovery proved to be a kind of deer hitherto unknown in	33	_____
Europe. The deer, already quite rare, had an ancient history in	44	_____
China. Legend said that they were harnessed to the chariots of	55	_____
Chinese gods.	57	_____
European zoos immediately wanted the deer, and China gave	66	_____
some away. Then in 1900 soldiers shot the remaining deer during	77	_____
a rebellion. There were no more Father David's deer in China.	88	_____
In England a British duke realized that European zoos had	98	_____
the only surviving Father David's deer. He bought them all—18	109	_____
of them—and set them loose on his estate. After he died, his son	123	_____
and then his grandson took over their care.	131	_____
In 1980 representatives of the Chinese government	138	_____
approached the duke's family in England. Might they have	147	_____
some of their native deer back? After much discussion, a plan	158	_____
was approved and a suitable place chosen. Chinese workers	167	_____
planted grass and built a high wall around the parkland where	178	_____
the deer would be released. In 1986, for the first time in 86	191	_____
years, 22 of China's native deer were back in China.	201	_____

Needs Work   1   2   3   4   5   Excellent
Paid attention to punctuation

Needs Work   1   2   3   4   5   Excellent
Sounded good

Total Words Read _____

Total Errors − _____

Correct WPM _____

36 Nonfiction

from *Growing Up*
by Russell Baker

First Reading

	Words Read	Miscues

She had always been a small woman—short, light-boned, · · · 9 · _____

delicately structured—but now, under the white hospital sheet, · · · 18 · _____

[my mother] was becoming tiny. I thought of a doll with huge, · · · 30 · _____

fierce eyes. There had always been fierceness in her. It showed · · · 41 · _____

in that angry, challenging thrust of the chin when she issued · · · 52 · _____

an opinion, and a great one she had always been for issuing · · · 64 · _____

opinions. · · · 65 · _____

"I tell people exactly what's on my mind," she had been fond · · · 77 · _____

of boasting. "I tell them what I think, whether they like it or not." · · · 91 · _____

Often they had not liked it. She could be sarcastic to people in · · · 104 · _____

whom she detected evidence of the ignoramus or the fool. · · · 114 · _____

"It's not always good policy to tell people exactly what's on · · · 125 · _____

your mind," I used to caution her. · · · 132 · _____

"If they don't like it, that's too bad," was her customary reply, · · · 144 · _____

"because that's the way I am." · · · 150 · _____

And so she was. A formidable woman. Determined to speak · · · 160 · _____

her mind, determined to have her way, determined to bend those · · · 171 · _____

who opposed her. In that time when I had known her best, my · · · 184 · _____

mother had hurled herself at life with chin thrust forward, eyes · · · 195 · _____

blazing, and an energy that made her seem always on the run. · · · 207 · _____

Needs Work   1 2 3 4 5   Excellent
Paid attention to punctuation

Needs Work   1 2 3 4 5   Excellent
Sounded good

Total Words Read _____

Total Errors − _____

Correct WPM _____

from *Growing Up*
by Russell Baker

	Words Read	Miscues
She had always been a small woman—short, light-boned,	9	_____
delicately structured—but now, under the white hospital sheet,	18	_____
[my mother] was becoming tiny. I thought of a doll with huge,	30	_____
fierce eyes. There had always been fierceness in her. It showed	41	_____
in that angry, challenging thrust of the chin when she issued	52	_____
an opinion, and a great one she had always been for issuing	64	_____
opinions.	65	_____
"I tell people exactly what's on my mind," she had been fond	77	_____
of boasting. "I tell them what I think, whether they like it or not."	91	_____
Often they had not liked it. She could be sarcastic to people in	104	_____
whom she detected evidence of the ignoramus or the fool.	114	_____
"It's not always good policy to tell people exactly what's on	125	_____
your mind," I used to caution her.	132	_____
"If they don't like it, that's too bad," was her customary reply,	144	_____
"because that's the way I am."	150	_____
And so she was. A formidable woman. Determined to speak	160	_____
her mind, determined to have her way, determined to bend those	171	_____
who opposed her. In that time when I had known her best, my	184	_____
mother had hurled herself at life with chin thrust forward, eyes	195	_____
blazing, and an energy that made her seem always on the run.	207	_____

Needs Work　1　2　3　4　5　Excellent
Paid attention to punctuation

Needs Work　1　2　3　4　5　Excellent
Sounded good

Total Words Read _____

Total Errors − _____

Correct WPM _____

37

Fiction

from *So Far from the Bamboo Grove*
by Yoko Kawashima Watkins

First Reading

	Words Read	Miscues

The pupils began digging ditches around the school in case   **10** _____

an air raid came and we had no time to get home. I was given a   **26** _____

shovel, but the handle was much taller than I and heavy. I could   **39** _____

not dig that hard rocky ground. I huffed and puffed, just wrestling   **51** _____

with the shovel.   **54** _____

We learned which siren was an alert and which an all-clear.   **65** _____

We were digging when our first air raid alarm came. The alert   **77** _____

siren burst out; our teacher, Mr. Enomoto, shouted, ordering   **86** _____

everyone to flatten on the ground. I heard engines roaring over   **97** _____

my head.   **99** _____

I had never seen an airplane, but when I looked up, I saw   **112** _____

clearly: American planes in formations of three flying over us.   **122** _____

Mr. Enomoto yelled at me to put my head down. His scream was   **135** _____

angry and frightening. My heart raced, and, face down, I breathed   **146** _____

heavily, my breath scattering the dirt around my mouth. When the   **157** _____

all-clear sounded I wanted to go home, but we continued to dig.   **169** _____

When I did get home I was exhausted, and I could not   **181** _____

concentrate on my calligraphy lesson. My hands were still   **190** _____

shaking. My first air raid experience, and Father was not home!   **201** _____

I felt very insecure.   **205** _____

Needs Work   1   2   3   4   5   Excellent
Paid attention to punctuation

Needs Work   1   2   3   4   5   Excellent
Sounded good

Total Words Read _____

Total Errors − _____

Correct WPM _____

from *So Far from the Bamboo Grove*
by Yoko Kawashima Watkins

	Words Read	Miscues
The pupils began digging ditches around the school in case	10	_____
an air raid came and we had no time to get home. I was given a	26	_____
shovel, but the handle was much taller than I and heavy. I could	39	_____
not dig that hard rocky ground. I huffed and puffed, just wrestling	51	_____
with the shovel.	54	_____
We learned which siren was an alert and which an all-clear.	65	_____
We were digging when our first air raid alarm came. The alert	77	_____
siren burst out; our teacher, Mr. Enomoto, shouted, ordering	86	_____
everyone to flatten on the ground. I heard engines roaring over	97	_____
my head.	99	_____
I had never seen an airplane, but when I looked up, I saw	112	_____
clearly: American planes in formations of three flying over us.	122	_____
Mr. Enomoto yelled at me to put my head down. His scream was	135	_____
angry and frightening. My heart raced, and, face down, I breathed	146	_____
heavily, my breath scattering the dirt around my mouth. When the	157	_____
all-clear sounded I wanted to go home, but we continued to dig.	169	_____
When I did get home I was exhausted, and I could not	181	_____
concentrate on my calligraphy lesson. My hands were still	190	_____
shaking. My first air raid experience, and Father was not home!	201	_____
I felt very insecure.	205	_____

Needs Work   1   2   3   4   5   Excellent
Paid attention to punctuation

Needs Work   1   2   3   4   5   Excellent
Sounded good

Total Words Read   _____

Total Errors   − _____

Correct WPM   _____

74

38 Close Call

Nonfiction

	Words Read	Miscues

High above the California desert, Kerri Hannum stood | 8 | _____
on a cliff edge under the bright pink wings of her hang glider. | 21 | _____
A moment later, she launched herself off the cliff, aiming for a | 33 | _____
thermal—a rising column of hot air. She hit it just right. All at | 47 | _____
once she was rising faster than 1,000 feet a minute! At 14,000 | 59 | _____
feet, above the desert floor, she angled out of the thermal. | 70 | _____

Suddenly, her breath was knocked out of her as a blast of | 82 | _____
heavy, cold air struck her. It bashed her downward with more | 93 | _____
force than she had ever encountered. Kerri fought to hold her | 104 | _____
glider steady. It was no use: the glider's nose was knocked from | 116 | _____
a three-o'clock position—level flight—through six o'clock—full | 125 | _____
dive. This had happened to Kerri before. Glider pilots called | 135 | _____
it "going over the falls." This time, however, Kerri's glider was | 146 | _____
shoved so hard that it pivoted on to nine o'clock—completely | 157 | _____
upside down! She was in danger of falling onto her glider and | 169 | _____
breaking its delicate structure of tubing and wires. | 177 | _____

As Kerri pulled hard on the control bar to shift her weight | 189 | _____
forward and gain airspeed, her glider sank back into a controllable | 200 | _____
dive. She breathed a sigh of relief as she soared on. | 211 | _____

Needs Work   1   2   3   4   5   Excellent
Paid attention to punctuation

Needs Work   1   2   3   4   5   Excellent
Sounded good

Total Words Read _____

Total Errors − _____

Correct WPM _____

Close Call

High above the California desert, Kerri Hannum stood   8   _____

on a cliff edge under the bright pink wings of her hang glider.   21   _____

A moment later, she launched herself off the cliff, aiming for a   33   _____

thermal—a rising column of hot air. She hit it just right. All at   47   _____

once she was rising faster than 1,000 feet a minute! At 14,000   59   _____

feet, above the desert floor, she angled out of the thermal.   70   _____

Suddenly, her breath was knocked out of her as a blast of   82   _____

heavy, cold air struck her. It bashed her downward with more   93   _____

force than she had ever encountered. Kerri fought to hold her   104   _____

glider steady. It was no use: the glider's nose was knocked from   116   _____

a three-o'clock position—level flight—through six o'clock—full   125   _____

dive. This had happened to Kerri before. Glider pilots called   135   _____

it "going over the falls." This time, however, Kerri's glider was   146   _____

shoved so hard that it pivoted on to nine o'clock—completely   157   _____

upside down! She was in danger of falling onto her glider and   169   _____

breaking its delicate structure of tubing and wires.   177   _____

As Kerri pulled hard on the control bar to shift her weight   189   _____

forward and gain airspeed, her glider sank back into a controllable   200   _____

dive. She breathed a sigh of relief as she soared on.   211   _____

Needs Work   1   2   3   4   5   Excellent
Paid attention to punctuation

Needs Work   1   2   3   4   5   Excellent
Sounded good

Total Words Read   _____

Total Errors   – _____

Correct WPM   _____

39

Fiction

from *Julie of the Wolves*
by Jean Craighead George

First Reading

	Words Read	Miscues

❖❖❖

	Words Read	Miscues
Miyax stared hard at the regal black wolf, hoping to catch his	12	_____
eye. She must somehow tell him that she was starving and ask	24	_____
him for food. This could be done she knew, for her father, an	37	_____
Eskimo hunter, had done so. One year he had camped near a	49	_____
wolf den while on a hunt. When a month had passed and her	62	_____
father had seen no game, he told the leader of the wolves that	75	_____
he was hungry and needed food. The next night the wolf called	87	_____
him from far away and her father went to him and found a freshly	101	_____
killed caribou. Unfortunately, Miyax's father never explained to	109	_____
her how he had told the wolf of his needs. And not long afterward	123	_____
he paddled his kayak into the Bering Sea to hunt for seal, and he	137	_____
never returned.	139	_____
She had been watching the wolves for two days, trying to	150	_____
discern which of their sounds and movements expressed goodwill	159	_____
and friendship. Most animals had such signals. The little Arctic	169	_____
ground squirrels flicked their tails sideways to notify others of	179	_____
their kind that they were friendly. By imitating this signal with	190	_____
her forefinger, Miyax had lured many a squirrel to her hand. If	202	_____
she could discover such a gesture for the wolves she would be	214	_____
able to make friends.	218	_____

Needs Work   1 2 3 4 5   Excellent
Paid attention to punctuation

Needs Work   1 2 3 4 5   Excellent
Sounded good

Total Words Read _____

Total Errors − _____

Correct WPM _____

39

Fiction

from *Julie of the Wolves*
by Jean Craighead George

Miyax stared hard at the regal black wolf, hoping to catch his	12	_____
eye. She must somehow tell him that she was starving and ask	24	_____
him for food. This could be done she knew, for her father, an	37	_____
Eskimo hunter, had done so. One year he had camped near a	49	_____
wolf den while on a hunt. When a month had passed and her	62	_____
father had seen no game, he told the leader of the wolves that	75	_____
he was hungry and needed food. The next night the wolf called	87	_____
him from far away and her father went to him and found a freshly	101	_____
killed caribou. Unfortunately, Miyax's father never explained to	109	_____
her how he had told the wolf of his needs. And not long afterward	123	_____
he paddled his kayak into the Bering Sea to hunt for seal, and he	137	_____
never returned.	139	_____
She had been watching the wolves for two days, trying to	150	_____
discern which of their sounds and movements expressed goodwill	159	_____
and friendship. Most animals had such signals. The little Arctic	169	_____
ground squirrels flicked their tails sideways to notify others of	179	_____
their kind that they were friendly. By imitating this signal with	190	_____
her forefinger, Miyax had lured many a squirrel to her hand. If	202	_____
she could discover such a gesture for the wolves she would be	214	_____
able to make friends.	218	_____

Needs Work   1   2   3   4   5   Excellent
　　　　　Paid attention to punctuation

Needs Work   1   2   3   4   5   Excellent
　　　　　Sounded good

Total Words Read _____

Total Errors − _____

Correct WPM _____

40
Fiction

from *Island of the Blue Dolphins*
by Scott O'Dell

First Reading

	Words Read	Miscues

By the time I filled the basket, the Aleut ship had sailed   12 _____
around the wide kelp bed that encloses our island and between   23 _____
the two rocks that guard Coral Cove. Word of its coming had   35 _____
already reached the village of Ghalas-at. Carrying their weapons,   44 _____
our men sped along the trail which winds down to the shore.   56 _____
Our women were gathering at the edge of the mesa.   66 _____

I made my way through the heavy brush and, moving swiftly,   77 _____
down the ravine until I came to the sea cliffs. There I crouched   90 _____
on my hands and knees. Below me lay the cove. The tide was   103 _____
out and the sun shone on the white sand of the beach. Half the   117 _____
men from our village stood at the water's edge. The rest were   129 _____
concealed among the rocks at the foot of the trail, ready to attack   142 _____
the intruders should they prove unfriendly.   148 _____

As I crouched there in the toyon bushes, trying not to fall   160 _____
over the cliff, trying to keep myself hidden and yet to see and   173 _____
hear what went on below me, a boat left the ship. Six men with   187 _____
long oars were rowing. Their faces were broad, and shining dark   198 _____
hair fell over their eyes. When they came closer I saw that they   211 _____
had bone ornaments thrust through their noses.   218 _____

Needs Work   1   2   3   4   5   Excellent
_____
Paid attention to punctuation

Needs Work   1   2   3   4   5   Excellent
_____
Sounded good

Total Words Read _____

Total Errors − _____

Correct WPM _____

40

Fiction

from *Island of the Blue Dolphins*
by Scott O'Dell

	Words Read	Miscues

By the time I filled the basket, the Aleut ship had sailed 　　12 ____

around the wide kelp bed that encloses our island and between 　　23 ____

the two rocks that guard Coral Cove. Word of its coming had 　　35 ____

already reached the village of Ghalas-at. Carrying their weapons, 　　44 ____

our men sped along the trail which winds down to the shore. 　　56 ____

Our women were gathering at the edge of the mesa. 　　66 ____

I made my way through the heavy brush and, moving swiftly, 　　77 ____

down the ravine until I came to the sea cliffs. There I crouched 　　90 ____

on my hands and knees. Below me lay the cove. The tide was 　　103 ____

out and the sun shone on the white sand of the beach. Half the 　　117 ____

men from our village stood at the water's edge. The rest were 　　129 ____

concealed among the rocks at the foot of the trail, ready to attack 　　142 ____

the intruders should they prove unfriendly. 　　148 ____

As I crouched there in the toyon bushes, trying not to fall 　　160 ____

over the cliff, trying to keep myself hidden and yet to see and 　　173 ____

hear what went on below me, a boat left the ship. Six men with 　　187 ____

long oars were rowing. Their faces were broad, and shining dark 　　198 ____

hair fell over their eyes. When they came closer I saw that they 　　211 ____

had bone ornaments thrust through their noses. 　　218 ____

Needs Work　1　2　3　4　5　Excellent

Paid attention to punctuation

Needs Work　1　2　3　4　5　Excellent

Sounded good

Total Words Read _____

Total Errors − _____

Correct WPM _____

Bouqui and Lapin, a Cajun Tale

Fiction

	Words Read	Miscues

One spring Bouqui and Lapin agreed to farm together. Lapin   10   _____
suggested that they divide everything equally. Bouqui would take   19   _____
the parts that grew under the ground, while he, Lapin, would   30   _____
take the parts that grew above the ground. Bouqui agreed. Lapin   41   _____
provided the seeds, and Bouqui did all of the plowing and planting.   53   _____

When the crops were ready for harvesting, Bouqui realized   62   _____
that the only parts underground were the roots of the plants.   73   _____
They had grown tomatoes, corn, beans, cabbage, and melons.   82   _____
Lapin consoled Bouqui by telling him that he could feed the   93   _____
roots to his cow.   97   _____

The next spring, Bouqui approached Lapin and suggested   105   _____
that they farm together again. However, this year he would take   116   _____
all the parts that grew above the ground, and Lapin would have   128   _____
the parts that grew under the ground. Lapin agreed. Once again   139   _____
Lapin provided the seeds, and Bouqui did all the plowing and   150   _____
the planting.   152   _____

Autumn came, and Bouqui discovered that the only parts   161   _____
aboveground were the leaves of the plants and some inedible   171   _____
gourds. They had grown yams, carrots, turnips, peanuts, and   180   _____
potatoes. Lapin consoled Bouqui by telling him that he could   190   _____
make fine dippers and bowls out of the gourds.   199   _____

Needs Work   1 2 3 4 5   Excellent
Paid attention to punctuation

Needs Work   1 2 3 4 5   Excellent
Sounded good

Total Words Read   _____

Total Errors   − _____

Correct WPM   _____

Bouqui and Lapin, a Cajun Tale

	Words Read	Miscues

One spring Bouqui and Lapin agreed to farm together. Lapin   10   _____

suggested that they divide everything equally. Bouqui would take   19   _____

the parts that grew under the ground, while he, Lapin, would   30   _____

take the parts that grew above the ground. Bouqui agreed. Lapin   41   _____

provided the seeds, and Bouqui did all of the plowing and planting.   53   _____

When the crops were ready for harvesting, Bouqui realized   62   _____

that the only parts underground were the roots of the plants.   73   _____

They had grown tomatoes, corn, beans, cabbage, and melons.   82   _____

Lapin consoled Bouqui by telling him that he could feed the   93   _____

roots to his cow.   97   _____

The next spring, Bouqui approached Lapin and suggested   105   _____

that they farm together again. However, this year he would take   116   _____

all the parts that grew above the ground, and Lapin would have   128   _____

the parts that grew under the ground. Lapin agreed. Once again   139   _____

Lapin provided the seeds, and Bouqui did all the plowing and   150   _____

the planting.   152   _____

Autumn came, and Bouqui discovered that the only parts   161   _____

aboveground were the leaves of the plants and some inedible   171   _____

gourds. They had grown yams, carrots, turnips, peanuts, and   180   _____

potatoes. Lapin consoled Bouqui by telling him that he could   190   _____

make fine dippers and bowls out of the gourds.   199   _____

Needs Work   1   2   3   4   5   Excellent
Paid attention to punctuation

Needs Work   1   2   3   4   5   Excellent
Sounded good

Total Words Read   _____

Total Errors   − _____

Correct WPM   _____

42

Nonfiction

Fingers of Discovery

	Words Read	Miscues

The forty sightless youngsters came down from the bus, full of — 11 — _____

questions and wonder. A few of the children with some sight could — 23 — _____

see the outline of an elephant or a donkey. But when it came to — 37 — _____

visiting a zoo, they, along with their totally blind friends, would — 48 — _____

use their hands and fingers to explore the forms of animal life. — 60 — _____

Guides seated the youngsters in the zoo's theater. Then one of — 71 — _____

them named the animals they would "see," described their habits, — 81 — _____

and answered the children's questions. — 86 — _____

Afterwards, other guides brought out stuffed owls and hawks, — 95 — _____

since live ones could not be handled, and let the young fingers — 107 — _____

discover the shape and form. The guides' comments were mostly — 117 — _____

about the sense of touch: "Doesn't he feel funny?" "Watch out for — 129 — _____

that sharp beak!" — 132 — _____

Later came the guinea pigs, turtles, and rabbits. They were — 142 — _____

a mixture of furs, feathers, shells, and hides, which delighted — 152 — _____

the group. — 154 — _____

Then the children were led into the contact area where they — 165 — _____

found larger animals. Here they were allowed to feed carrots to — 176 — _____

the goats, pet the lambs and calves, and feel the animals' wool — 188 — _____

and horns. — 190 — _____

After two hours, the youngsters grew tired. This time of — 200 — _____

exploration and learning had been an adventure. — 207 — _____

Needs Work   1   2   3   4   5   Excellent
Paid attention to punctuation

Needs Work   1   2   3   4   5   Excellent
Sounded good

Total Words Read _____

Total Errors – _____

Correct WPM _____

Fingers of Discovery

	Words Read	Miscues

The forty sightless youngsters came down from the bus, full of | 11 | _____
questions and wonder. A few of the children with some sight could | 23 | _____
see the outline of an elephant or a donkey. But when it came to | 37 | _____
visiting a zoo, they, along with their totally blind friends, would | 48 | _____
use their hands and fingers to explore the forms of animal life. | 60 | _____

Guides seated the youngsters in the zoo's theater. Then one of | 71 | _____
them named the animals they would "see," described their habits, | 81 | _____
and answered the children's questions. | 86 | _____

Afterwards, other guides brought out stuffed owls and hawks, | 95 | _____
since live ones could not be handled, and let the young fingers | 107 | _____
discover the shape and form. The guides' comments were mostly | 117 | _____
about the sense of touch: "Doesn't he feel funny?" "Watch out for | 129 | _____
that sharp beak!" | 132 | _____

Later came the guinea pigs, turtles, and rabbits. They were | 142 | _____
a mixture of furs, feathers, shells, and hides, which delighted | 152 | _____
the group. | 154 | _____

Then the children were led into the contact area where they | 165 | _____
found larger animals. Here they were allowed to feed carrots to | 176 | _____
the goats, pet the lambs and calves, and feel the animals' wool | 188 | _____
and horns. | 190 | _____

After two hours, the youngsters grew tired. This time of | 200 | _____
exploration and learning had been an adventure. | 207 | _____

Needs Work   1 2 3 4 5   Excellent
Paid attention to punctuation

Needs Work   1 2 3 4 5   Excellent
Sounded good

Total Words Read _____

Total Errors − _____

Correct WPM _____

43

Nonfiction

from *Barrio Boy*
by Ernesto Galarza

	Words Read	Miscues

The two of us walked south on Fifth Street one morning to   12 _____

the corner of Q Street and turned right. Half of the block was   25 _____

occupied by the Lincoln School. It was a three-story wooden   35 _____

building, with two wings that gave it the shape of a double-T   47 _____

connected by a central hall. It was a new building, painted yellow,   59 _____

with a shingled roof that was not like the red tile of the school in   74 _____

Mazatlán. I noticed other differences, none of them very reassuring.   84 _____

We walked up the wide staircase hand in hand and through   95 _____

the door, which closed by itself. A mechanical contraption   104 _____

screwed to the top shut it behind us quietly.   113 _____

Up to this point the adventure of enrolling me in the school   125 _____

had been carefully rehearsed. Mrs. Dodson had told us how to   136 _____

find it and we had circled it several times on our walks. Friends in   150 _____

the *barrio* explained that the director was called a principal, and   161 _____

that it was a lady and not a man. They assured us that there was   176 _____

always a person at the school who could speak Spanish.   186 _____

Exactly as we had been told, there was a sign on the door in   200 _____

both Spanish and English: "Principal." We crossed the hall and   210 _____

entered the office of Miss Nettie Hopley.   217 _____

Needs Work   1   2   3   4   5   Excellent
_____
Paid attention to punctuation

Needs Work   1   2   3   4   5   Excellent
_____
Sounded good

Total Words Read _____

Total Errors − _____

Correct WPM _____

43

Nonfiction

from *Barrio Boy*
by Ernesto Galarza

	Words Read	Miscues

The two of us walked south on Fifth Street one morning to — 12 — _____

the corner of Q Street and turned right. Half of the block was — 25 — _____

occupied by the Lincoln School. It was a three-story wooden — 35 — _____

building, with two wings that gave it the shape of a double-T — 47 — _____

connected by a central hall. It was a new building, painted yellow, — 59 — _____

with a shingled roof that was not like the red tile of the school in — 74 — _____

Mazatlán. I noticed other differences, none of them very reassuring. — 84 — _____

We walked up the wide staircase hand in hand and through — 95 — _____

the door, which closed by itself. A mechanical contraption — 104 — _____

screwed to the top shut it behind us quietly. — 113 — _____

Up to this point the adventure of enrolling me in the school — 125 — _____

had been carefully rehearsed. Mrs. Dodson had told us how to — 136 — _____

find it and we had circled it several times on our walks. Friends in — 150 — _____

the *barrio* explained that the director was called a principal, and — 161 — _____

that it was a lady and not a man. They assured us that there was — 176 — _____

always a person at the school who could speak Spanish. — 186 — _____

Exactly as we had been told, there was a sign on the door in — 200 — _____

both Spanish and English: "Principal." We crossed the hall and — 210 — _____

entered the office of Miss Nettie Hopley. — 217 — _____

Needs Work   1 2 3 4 5   Excellent

Paid attention to punctuation

Needs Work   1 2 3 4 5   Excellent

Sounded good

Total Words Read _____

Total Errors − _____

Correct WPM _____

44

Fiction

from "The Rockpile"
by James Baldwin

First Reading

	Words Read	Miscues

John watched [Roy] sourly as he carefully unlocked the door | 10 | _____
and disappeared. In a moment he saw him on the sidewalk with | 22 | _____
his friends. He did not dare to go and tell his mother that Roy | 36 | _____
had left the fire escape because he had practically promised not | 47 | _____
to. He started to shout, *Remember, you said five minutes!* but one | 59 | _____
of Roy's friends was looking up at the fire escape. John looked | 71 | _____
down at his schoolbook: he became engrossed again in the | 81 | _____
problem of the locomotive. | 85 | _____

When he looked up again he did not know how much time | 97 | _____
had passed, but now there was a gang fight on the rockpile. | 109 | _____
Dozens of boys fought each other in the harsh sun: clambering | 120 | _____
up the rocks and battling hand to hand, scuffed shoes sliding on | 132 | _____
the slippery rock; filling the bright air with curses and jubilant | 143 | _____
cries. They filled the air, too, with flying weapons: stones, sticks, | 154 | _____
tin cans, garbage, whatever could be picked up and thrown. John | 165 | _____
watched in a kind of absent amazement—until he remembered | 175 | _____
that Roy was still downstairs, and that he was one of the boys | 188 | _____
on the rockpile. Then he was afraid; he could not see his brother | 201 | _____
among the figures in the sun; and he stood up, leaning over the | 214 | _____
fire-escape railing. | 216 | _____

Needs Work   1   2   3   4   5   Excellent
Paid attention to punctuation

Needs Work   1   2   3   4   5   Excellent
Sounded good

Total Words Read _____

Total Errors − _____

Correct WPM _____

44

Fiction

from "The Rockpile"

by James Baldwin

	Words Read	Miscues

John watched [Roy] sourly as he carefully unlocked the door | 10 | _____

and disappeared. In a moment he saw him on the sidewalk with | 22 | _____

his friends. He did not dare to go and tell his mother that Roy | 36 | _____

had left the fire escape because he had practically promised not | 47 | _____

to. He started to shout, *Remember, you said five minutes!* but one | 59 | _____

of Roy's friends was looking up at the fire escape. John looked | 71 | _____

down at his schoolbook: he became engrossed again in the | 81 | _____

problem of the locomotive. | 85 | _____

When he looked up again he did not know how much time | 97 | _____

had passed, but now there was a gang fight on the rockpile. | 109 | _____

Dozens of boys fought each other in the harsh sun: clambering | 120 | _____

up the rocks and battling hand to hand, scuffed shoes sliding on | 132 | _____

the slippery rock; filling the bright air with curses and jubilant | 143 | _____

cries. They filled the air, too, with flying weapons: stones, sticks, | 154 | _____

tin cans, garbage, whatever could be picked up and thrown. John | 165 | _____

watched in a kind of absent amazement—until he remembered | 175 | _____

that Roy was still downstairs, and that he was one of the boys | 188 | _____

on the rockpile. Then he was afraid; he could not see his brother | 201 | _____

among the figures in the sun; and he stood up, leaning over the | 214 | _____

fire-escape railing. | 216 | _____

Needs Work   1   2   3   4   5   Excellent
Paid attention to punctuation

Needs Work   1   2   3   4   5   Excellent
Sounded good

Total Words Read _____

Total Errors − _____

Correct WPM _____

45
Fiction

from *The Call of the Wild*
by Jack London

	Words Read	Miscues

The dogs were tired, the drivers grumbling, and to make | 10 | _____

matters worse, it snowed every day. This meant a soft trail, greater | 22 | _____

friction on the runners, and heavier pulling for the dogs; yet the | 34 | _____

drivers were fair through it all, and did their best for the animals. | 47 | _____

Each night the dogs were attended to first. They ate before the | 59 | _____

drivers ate, and no man sought his sleeping robe till he had seen | 72 | _____

to the feet of the dogs he drove. Still, their strength went down. | 85 | _____

Since the beginning of the winter they had traveled eighteen | 95 | _____

hundred miles, dragging sleds the whole weary distance; and | 104 | _____

eighteen hundred miles will tell upon the life of the toughest. | 115 | _____

[Among the sled dogs,] Buck stood it, though he too was very | 127 | _____

tired. Billee cried and whimpered regularly in his sleep each night. | 138 | _____

Joe was sourer than ever, and Sol-leks was unapproachable. | 147 | _____

But it was Dave who suffered most of all. Something had gone | 159 | _____

wrong with him. He became more morose and irritable, and when | 170 | _____

camp was pitched at once made his nest, where his driver fed | 182 | _____

him. Once out of the harness and down, he did not get on his | 196 | _____

feet again till harness-up time in the morning. | 204 | _____

Needs Work   1   2   3   4   5   Excellent
Paid attention to punctuation

Needs Work   1   2   3   4   5   Excellent
Sounded good

Total Words Read   _____

Total Errors − _____

Correct WPM   _____

45

Fiction

from *The Call of the Wild*
by Jack London

The dogs were tired, the drivers grumbling, and to make	10
matters worse, it snowed every day. This meant a soft trail, greater	22
friction on the runners, and heavier pulling for the dogs; yet the	34
drivers were fair through it all, and did their best for the animals.	47
Each night the dogs were attended to first. They ate before the	59
drivers ate, and no man sought his sleeping robe till he had seen	72
to the feet of the dogs he drove. Still, their strength went down.	85
Since the beginning of the winter they had traveled eighteen	95
hundred miles, dragging sleds the whole weary distance; and	104
eighteen hundred miles will tell upon the life of the toughest.	115
[Among the sled dogs,] Buck stood it, though he too was very	127
tired. Billee cried and whimpered regularly in his sleep each night.	138
Joe was sourer than ever, and Sol-leks was unapproachable.	147
But it was Dave who suffered most of all. Something had gone	159
wrong with him. He became more morose and irritable, and when	170
camp was pitched at once made his nest, where his driver fed	182
him. Once out of the harness and down, he did not get on his	196
feet again till harness-up time in the morning.	204

Needs Work   1   2   3   4   5   Excellent
Paid attention to punctuation

Needs Work   1   2   3   4   5   Excellent
Sounded good

Total Words Read _____

Total Errors − _____

Correct WPM _____

46

Fiction

from *Little Women*

by Louisa May Alcott

First Reading

	Words Read	Miscues

≈≈≈

"Merry Christmas, little daughters!" said Mrs. March. "I'm   8   _____

glad you began [enjoying your presents] at once, and hope you   19   _____

will keep on. But I want to say one word before we sit down [to   34   _____

breakfast]. Not far away from here lies a poor woman with a little   47   _____

newborn baby. Six children are huddled into one bed to keep   58   _____

from freezing, for they have no fire. There is nothing to eat over   71   _____

there, and the oldest boy came to tell me they were suffering from   84   _____

hunger and cold. My girls, will you give them your breakfast as a   97   _____

Christmas present?"   99   _____

They were all unusually hungry, having waited nearly an hour,   109   _____

and for a minute no one spoke—only a minute, for Jo exclaimed,   122   _____

"I'm so glad you came before we began!"   130   _____

"May I go and help carry the things to the poor little children?"   143   _____

asked Beth.   145   _____

"I shall take the cream and the muffins," added Amy, heroically   156   _____

giving up the articles she most liked.   163   _____

Meg was already covering the buckwheats, and piling the bread   173   _____

into one big plate.   177   _____

"I thought you'd do it," said Mrs. March, smiling. "You shall   188   _____

all go and help me. When we come back we will have bread and   202   _____

milk for breakfast, and make it up at dinnertime."   211   _____

Needs Work   1   2   3   4   5   Excellent
Paid attention to punctuation

Needs Work   1   2   3   4   5   Excellent
Sounded good

Total Words Read   _____

Total Errors   − _____

Correct WPM   _____

46

Fiction

from *Little Women*
by Louisa May Alcott

	Words Read	Miscues

"Merry Christmas, little daughters!" said Mrs. March. "I'm   8   _____
glad you began [enjoying your presents] at once, and hope you   19   _____
will keep on. But I want to say one word before we sit down [to   34   _____
breakfast]. Not far away from here lies a poor woman with a little   47   _____
newborn baby. Six children are huddled into one bed to keep   58   _____
from freezing, for they have no fire. There is nothing to eat over   71   _____
there, and the oldest boy came to tell me they were suffering from   84   _____
hunger and cold. My girls, will you give them your breakfast as a   97   _____
Christmas present?"   99   _____

They were all unusually hungry, having waited nearly an hour,   109   _____
and for a minute no one spoke—only a minute, for Jo exclaimed,   122   _____
"I'm so glad you came before we began!"   130   _____

"May I go and help carry the things to the poor little children?"   143   _____
asked Beth.   145   _____

"I shall take the cream and the muffins," added Amy, heroically   156   _____
giving up the articles she most liked.   163   _____

Meg was already covering the buckwheats, and piling the bread   173   _____
into one big plate.   177   _____

"I thought you'd do it," said Mrs. March, smiling. "You shall   188   _____
all go and help me. When we come back we will have bread and   202   _____
milk for breakfast, and make it up at dinnertime."   211   _____

Needs Work   1   2   3   4   5   Excellent
Paid attention to punctuation

Needs Work   1   2   3   4   5   Excellent
Sounded good

Total Words Read _____

Total Errors − _____

Correct WPM _____

from "Lob's Girl"
by Joan Aiken

Fiction

	Words Read	Miscues

It became noticeable that a dog seemed to have taken up | 11 | _____

position outside the hospital, with the fixed intention of getting | 21 | _____

in. Patiently he would try first one entrance and then another, all | 33 | _____

the way around, and then begin again. Sometimes he would get | 44 | _____

a little way inside, following a visitor, but animals were, of course, | 56 | _____

forbidden, and he was always kindly but firmly turned out again. | 67 | _____

Sometimes the guard at the main entrance gave him a pat or | 79 | _____

offered him a bit of sandwich—he looked so wet and beseeching | 91 | _____

and desperate. But he never ate the sandwich. No one seemed to | 103 | _____

own him or to know where he came from: Plymouth is a large city | 117 | _____

and he might have belonged to anybody. | 124 | _____

At tea time Granny Pearce came through the pouring rain to | 135 | _____

bring a flask of hot tea with brandy in it to her daughter and son- | 150 | _____

in-law. Just as she reached the main entrance the guard was gently | 161 | _____

but forcibly shoving out a large, agitated, soaking-wet Alsatian dog. | 171 | _____

"No, old fellow, you can *not* come in. Hospitals are for people, | 183 | _____

not for dogs." | 186 | _____

"Why, bless me," exclaimed old Mrs. Pearce. "That's Lob! Here, | 196 | _____

Lob. Lobby boy!" | 199 | _____

Lob ran to her, whining. Mrs. Pearce walked up to the desk. | 211 | _____

"I'm sorry, madam, you can't bring that dog in here," the | 222 | _____

guard said. | 224 | _____

Needs Work   1 2 3 4 5   Excellent
Paid attention to punctuation

Needs Work   1 2 3 4 5   Excellent
Sounded good

Total Words Read _____

Total Errors − _____

Correct WPM _____

47

Fiction

from **"Lob's Girl"**

by Joan Aiken

It became noticeable that a dog seemed to have taken up	11
position outside the hospital, with the fixed intention of getting	21
in. Patiently he would try first one entrance and then another, all	33
the way around, and then begin again. Sometimes he would get	44
a little way inside, following a visitor, but animals were, of course,	56
forbidden, and he was always kindly but firmly turned out again.	67
Sometimes the guard at the main entrance gave him a pat or	79
offered him a bit of sandwich—he looked so wet and beseeching	91
and desperate. But he never ate the sandwich. No one seemed to	103
own him or to know where he came from: Plymouth is a large city	117
and he might have belonged to anybody.	124

At tea time Granny Pearce came through the pouring rain to · 135
bring a flask of hot tea with brandy in it to her daughter and son- · 150
in-law. Just as she reached the main entrance the guard was gently · 161
but forcibly shoving out a large, agitated, soaking-wet Alsatian dog. · 171

"No, old fellow, you can *not* come in. Hospitals are for people, · 183
not for dogs." · 186

"Why, bless me," exclaimed old Mrs. Pearce. "That's Lob! Here, · 196
Lob. Lobby boy!" · 199

Lob ran to her, whining. Mrs. Pearce walked up to the desk. · 211

"I'm sorry, madam, you can't bring that dog in here," the · 222
guard said. · 224

48 from "My Fights with Jack Dempsey"

Nonfiction

by Gene Tunney

〜〜〜〜

First Reading

	Words Read	Miscues

I had learned that [fighter Jack Dempsey's] trainers had been | 10 | _____

giving him special exercises for footwork, because he had slowed | 20 | _____

down in the legs. That was the cue—match my legs against his, | 33 | _____

keep away from him, depend on speed of foot, let him chase me | 46 | _____

until I was sure I had recovered completely from the knock-down. | 57 | _____

The plan would work if my own legs were in good shape, after | 70 | _____

the battering I had taken. That was what I had to think about on | 84 | _____

the floor in Chicago. My legs felt all right. At the count of nine I | 99 | _____

got up. My legs felt strong and springy. | 107 | _____

Jack came tearing in for the kill. I stepped away from him, | 119 | _____

moving to my left—circling away from his left hook. As I side- | 132 | _____

stepped swiftly, my legs had never been better. What I had heard | 143 | _____

about Dempsey's legs was true. As I circled away from him, he | 155 | _____

tried doggedly, desperately, to keep up with me—but he was slow. | 167 | _____

The strategy was okay—keep away from him until I was certain | 179 | _____

that all the effects of the knock-down had worn off. Once, in | 191 | _____

sheer desperation, Jack stopped in his tracks and growled at me | 202 | _____

to stand and fight. | 206 | _____

Needs Work   1   2   3   4   5   Excellent
Paid attention to punctuation

Needs Work   1   2   3   4   5   Excellent
Sounded good

Total Words Read _____

Total Errors − _____

Correct WPM _____

from "My Fights with Jack Dempsey"

by Gene Tunney

	Words Read	Miscues

I had learned that [fighter Jack Dempsey's] trainers had been | 10 | _____
giving him special exercises for footwork, because he had slowed | 20 | _____
down in the legs. That was the cue—match my legs against his, | 33 | _____
keep away from him, depend on speed of foot, let him chase me | 46 | _____
until I was sure I had recovered completely from the knock-down. | 57 | _____

The plan would work if my own legs were in good shape, after | 70 | _____
the battering I had taken. That was what I had to think about on | 84 | _____
the floor in Chicago. My legs felt all right. At the count of nine I | 99 | _____
got up. My legs felt strong and springy. | 107 | _____

Jack came tearing in for the kill. I stepped away from him, | 119 | _____
moving to my left—circling away from his left hook. As I side- | 132 | _____
stepped swiftly, my legs had never been better. What I had heard | 143 | _____
about Dempsey's legs was true. As I circled away from him, he | 155 | _____
tried doggedly, desperately, to keep up with me—but he was slow. | 167 | _____
The strategy was okay—keep away from him until I was certain | 179 | _____
that all the effects of the knock-down had worn off. Once, in | 191 | _____
sheer desperation, Jack stopped in his tracks and growled at me | 202 | _____
to stand and fight. | 206 | _____

Needs Work   1   2   3   4   5   Excellent
Paid attention to punctuation

Needs Work   1   2   3   4   5   Excellent
Sounded good

Total Words Read _____

Total Errors − _____

Correct WPM _____

49

Nonfiction

from *Traitor:*
The Case of Benedict Arnold
by Jean Fritz

First Reading

	Words Read	Miscues

⦸

	Words Read	Miscues
The town was in flames and there was nothing [the American	11	_____
troops] could do. Still, they had no intention of letting the British	23	_____
off free. The next day they would fight them on their way back to	37	_____
Norwalk. [General] Wooster would attack from the rear; [General]	46	_____
Arnold would meet the enemy head-on as they approached.	55	_____
Long before daylight Arnold and three hundred men were	64	_____
on their way. At Ridgefield Arnold picked the battle site—a spot	76	_____
where the road was squeezed between a rocky ledge on one side	88	_____
and a big farmhouse on the other. With the help of local residents,	101	_____
Arnold's men piled furniture, wheelbarrows, wagons, carts, lumber	109	_____
across the road to form a barricade. When they were done, Benedict	121	_____
Arnold, astride his horse, took a position in the center of the road	134	_____
behind the barricade and waited. As soon as he heard firing, he	146	_____
knew that Wooster had attacked. It would be his turn next.	157	_____
Then down the road came the British. An unending column,	167	_____
three abreast. Tramping, tramping as if nothing would or could	177	_____
stop them. And what could? Three hundred men against two	187	_____
thousand. And only a ramshackle barricade between them.	195	_____
Anyone would have said the American position was impossible,	204	_____
but then Benedict Arnold thrived on the impossible.	212	_____

Needs Work   1 2 3 4 5   Excellent
_____
Paid attention to punctuation

Needs Work   1 2 3 4 5   Excellent
_____
Sounded good

Total Words Read _____

Total Errors − _____

Correct WPM _____

97

from *Traitor:*

The Case of Benedict Arnold

by Jean Fritz

	Words Read	Miscues
The town was in flames and there was nothing [the American	11	_____
troops] could do. Still, they had no intention of letting the British	23	_____
off free. The next day they would fight them on their way back to	37	_____
Norwalk. [General] Wooster would attack from the rear; [General]	46	_____
Arnold would meet the enemy head-on as they approached.	55	_____
Long before daylight Arnold and three hundred men were	64	_____
on their way. At Ridgefield Arnold picked the battle site—a spot	76	_____
where the road was squeezed between a rocky ledge on one side	88	_____
and a big farmhouse on the other. With the help of local residents,	101	_____
Arnold's men piled furniture, wheelbarrows, wagons, carts, lumber	109	_____
across the road to form a barricade. When they were done, Benedict	121	_____
Arnold, astride his horse, took a position in the center of the road	134	_____
behind the barricade and waited. As soon as he heard firing, he	146	_____
knew that Wooster had attacked. It would be his turn next.	157	_____
Then down the road came the British. An unending column,	167	_____
three abreast. Tramping, tramping as if nothing would or could	177	_____
stop them. And what could? Three hundred men against two	187	_____
thousand. And only a ramshackle barricade between them.	195	_____
Anyone would have said the American position was impossible,	204	_____
but then Benedict Arnold thrived on the impossible.	212	_____

Needs Work   1   2   3   4   5   Excellent
Paid attention to punctuation

Needs Work   1   2   3   4   5   Excellent
Sounded good

Total Words Read _____

Total Errors − _____

Correct WPM _____

50

Fiction

from "Bad Influence"
by Judith Ortiz Cofer

First Reading

	Words Read	Miscues

Somehow we got out of the house before the sun came up | 12 | _____

and sandwiched ourselves into the subcompact, whose muffler | 20 | _____

must have woken up half the island. Why doesn't anyone ever | 31 | _____

mention noise pollution around here? was my last thought before | 41 | _____

I fell asleep crunched up in the backseat. | 49 | _____

When I opened my eyes, I was blinded by the glare of the | 62 | _____

sun coming through the car windows; and when my eyeballs | 72 | _____

came back into their sockets, I saw that we had pulled up at the | 86 | _____

side of a house right on the beach. This was no ordinary house. | 99 | _____

It looked like a huge pink-and-white birthday cake. No joke—it | 110 | _____

was painted baby pink with white trim and a white roof. It had | 123 | _____

a terrace that went all the way around it, so that it really did look | 138 | _____

like a layer cake. If I could afford a house like that, I would paint | 153 | _____

it a more serious color. Like purple. But around here, everyone | 164 | _____

is crazy about pastels: lime green, baby pink and blue—nursery | 175 | _____

school colors. | 177 | _____

The ocean was incredible, though. It was just a few yards | 188 | _____

away and it looked unreal. The water was turquoise in some | 199 | _____

places and dark blue, almost black, in others. | 207 | _____

Needs Work   1   2   3   4   5   Excellent
Paid attention to punctuation

Needs Work   1   2   3   4   5   Excellent
Sounded good

Total Words Read _____

Total Errors − _____

Correct WPM _____

from **"Bad Influence"**
by Judith Ortiz Cofer

	Words Read	Miscues

Somehow we got out of the house before the sun came up 12 _____
and sandwiched ourselves into the subcompact, whose muffler 20 _____
must have woken up half the island. Why doesn't anyone ever 31 _____
mention noise pollution around here? was my last thought before 41 _____
I fell asleep crunched up in the backseat. 49 _____

When I opened my eyes, I was blinded by the glare of the 62 _____
sun coming through the car windows; and when my eyeballs 72 _____
came back into their sockets, I saw that we had pulled up at the 86 _____
side of a house right on the beach. This was no ordinary house. 99 _____
It looked like a huge pink-and-white birthday cake. No joke—it 110 _____
was painted baby pink with white trim and a white roof. It had 123 _____
a terrace that went all the way around it, so that it really did look 138 _____
like a layer cake. If I could afford a house like that, I would paint 153 _____
it a more serious color. Like purple. But around here, everyone 164 _____
is crazy about pastels: lime green, baby pink and blue—nursery 175 _____
school colors. 177 _____

The ocean was incredible, though. It was just a few yards 188 _____
away and it looked unreal. The water was turquoise in some 199 _____
places and dark blue, almost black, in others. 207 _____

Needs Work   1   2   3   4   5   Excellent
Paid attention to punctuation

Needs Work   1   2   3   4   5   Excellent
Sounded good

Total Words Read _____

Total Errors − _____

Correct WPM _____

51

Fiction

from *Tortuga*
by Rudolfo A. Anaya

	Words Read	Miscues

A friend behind me whispered that if we were in luck there would | 13 | _____ |
be a deer drinking at the river. No one had ever killed a deer in | 28 | _____ |
the memory of our tribe. We held our breath and waited, until the | 41 | _____ |
leader motioned and I moved forward to see. There in the middle | 53 | _____ |
of the narrow path lay the biggest tortoise any of us had ever | 66 | _____ |
seen. It was a huge monster which had crawled out of the dark | 79 | _____ |
river to lay its eggs in the warm sand. I felt a shiver when I saw it, | 96 | _____ |
and when I breathed I smelled . . . the sea. The taste of copper | 108 | _____ |
drained in my mouth and settled in my queasy stomach. | 118 | _____ |

The giant turtle lifted its huge head and looked at us with dull, | 131 | _____ |
glintless eyes. The tribe drew back. Only I remained facing the | 142 | _____ |
monster from the water. Its slimy head dripped with bright green | 153 | _____ |
algae. It hissed a warning, asking me to move. It had come out of | 167 | _____ |
the water to lay its eggs, now it had to return to the river. Wet, | 182 | _____ |
leathery eggs fresh from the laying clung to its webbed feet, and | 194 | _____ |
as it moved forward it crushed them into the sand. Its gray shell | 207 | _____ |
was dry, dulled by the sun, encrusted with dead parasites and | 218 | _____ |
green growth; it needed the water. | 224 | _____ |

Needs Work   1   2   3   4   5   Excellent
Paid attention to punctuation

Needs Work   1   2   3   4   5   Excellent
Sounded good

Total Words Read _____

Total Errors − _____

Correct WPM _____

from *Tortuga*
by Rudolfo A. Anaya

	Words Read	Miscues
A friend behind me whispered that if we were in luck there would	13	_____
be a deer drinking at the river. No one had ever killed a deer in	28	_____
the memory of our tribe. We held our breath and waited, until the	41	_____
leader motioned and I moved forward to see. There in the middle	53	_____
of the narrow path lay the biggest tortoise any of us had ever	66	_____
seen. It was a huge monster which had crawled out of the dark	79	_____
river to lay its eggs in the warm sand. I felt a shiver when I saw it,	96	_____
and when I breathed I smelled . . . the sea. The taste of copper	108	_____
drained in my mouth and settled in my queasy stomach.	118	_____
The giant turtle lifted its huge head and looked at us with dull,	131	_____
glintless eyes. The tribe drew back. Only I remained facing the	142	_____
monster from the water. Its slimy head dripped with bright green	153	_____
algae. It hissed a warning, asking me to move. It had come out of	167	_____
the water to lay its eggs, now it had to return to the river. Wet,	182	_____
leathery eggs fresh from the laying clung to its webbed feet, and	194	_____
as it moved forward it crushed them into the sand. Its gray shell	207	_____
was dry, dulled by the sun, encrusted with dead parasites and	218	_____
green growth; it needed the water.	224	_____

Needs Work   1   2   3   4   5   Excellent
Paid attention to punctuation

Needs Work   1   2   3   4   5   Excellent
Sounded good

Total Words Read _____

Total Errors − _____

Correct WPM _____

52
Nonfiction

Koko's Kitten

First Reading

	Words Read	Miscues

〰〰〰

Can a gorilla love a kitten? One 230-pound lowland gorilla | 10 | _____

named Koko did. Koko was part of a study in which gorillas were | 23 | _____

taught American Sign Language, the system of communication | 31 | _____

used by many hearing-impaired people. Koko learned and used | 40 | _____

more than 500 signs and understood another 500 signs. | 49 | _____

Koko was fascinated by cats. "The Three Little Kittens" and | 59 | _____

"Puss in Boots" were two of her favorite stories. One day Koko | 71 | _____

signed to her trainer, Dr. Francine Patterson, that she wanted a | 82 | _____

cat. Dr. Patterson gave Koko a toy cat, but she just pouted. It was | 96 | _____

obvious that this was not what Koko had meant. When someone | 107 | _____

brought three abandoned kittens to the center where Koko lived, | 117 | _____

Koko signed, "Love that," so Dr. Patterson let her pick one for a | 130 | _____

pet. Koko's choice was a male kitten with no tail. She named him | 143 | _____

All Ball. | 145 | _____

Koko treated her kitten as she would have treated a baby | 156 | _____

gorilla. She carried him tucked against herself or held him gently | 167 | _____

and petted him. As a child would, she even dressed her pet in | 180 | _____

napkins and hats! The huge gorilla and the tiny kitten enjoyed | 191 | _____

playing chase together, as well as Koko's favorite game, tickling. | 201 | _____

As Koko held her pet, she often signed, "Soft good cat cat." | 213 | _____

Needs Work   1 2 3 4 5   Excellent
Paid attention to punctuation

Needs Work   1 2 3 4 5   Excellent
Sounded good

Total Words Read _____

Total Errors − _____

Correct WPM _____

Koko's Kitten

52

Nonfiction

	Words Read	Miscues

Can a gorilla love a kitten? One 230-pound lowland gorilla — 10 _____

named Koko did. Koko was part of a study in which gorillas were — 23 _____

taught American Sign Language, the system of communication — 31 _____

used by many hearing-impaired people. Koko learned and used — 40 _____

more than 500 signs and understood another 500 signs. — 49 _____

Koko was fascinated by cats. "The Three Little Kittens" and — 59 _____

"Puss in Boots" were two of her favorite stories. One day Koko — 71 _____

signed to her trainer, Dr. Francine Patterson, that she wanted a — 82 _____

cat. Dr. Patterson gave Koko a toy cat, but she just pouted. It was — 96 _____

obvious that this was not what Koko had meant. When someone — 107 _____

brought three abandoned kittens to the center where Koko lived, — 117 _____

Koko signed, "Love that," so Dr. Patterson let her pick one for a — 130 _____

pet. Koko's choice was a male kitten with no tail. She named him — 143 _____

All Ball. — 145 _____

Koko treated her kitten as she would have treated a baby — 156 _____

gorilla. She carried him tucked against herself or held him gently — 167 _____

and petted him. As a child would, she even dressed her pet in — 180 _____

napkins and hats! The huge gorilla and the tiny kitten enjoyed — 191 _____

playing chase together, as well as Koko's favorite game, tickling. — 201 _____

As Koko held her pet, she often signed, "Soft good cat cat." — 213 _____

Needs Work 1 2 3 4 5 Excellent
Paid attention to punctuation

Needs Work 1 2 3 4 5 Excellent
Sounded good

Total Words Read _____

Total Errors − _____

Correct WPM _____

53 Hawaiian Hurricane

Nonfiction

First Reading

	Words Read	Miscues

On September 11, 1993, Hurricane Iniki, which had been — 9 _____

moving along a harmless path, took a sharp turn, headed north, — 20 _____

and made its way straight for Hawaii. Gaining strength as it went, — 32 _____

the storm carried torrential rains and wind gusts up to 180 miles — 44 _____

per hour. — 46 _____

The hurricane dealt only a glancing blow to most of the — 57 _____

Hawaiian islands. But Iniki hit Kauai with its full force. The — 68 _____

eye of the storm passed right over the island. — 77 _____

The roofs on thousands of buildings on the island were blown — 88 _____

away or damaged. Other buildings were completely destroyed. — 96 _____

The storm flattened fields of sugar cane. It toppled rows of — 107 _____

hardwood trees. It also created monstrous 20-foot ocean waves. — 116 _____

These swept cars away. The waves eroded beaches and washed — 126 _____

out coastal roads. Boats anchored at Port Allen Harbor were — 136 _____

piled up on top of each other. — 143 _____

Iniki also threatened tourists trapped on the island. The — 152 _____

hurricane blasted their hotels. Guests were forced to flee inland — 162 _____

and wait in long lines at grocery stores to buy food and water. The — 176 _____

damage to Kauai's luxury hotels was so extensive that nine months — 187 _____

after the hurricane only four of the 11 hotels had reopened. — 198 _____

The governor of Hawaii said it was probably the worst disaster — 209 _____

in the history of the state. — 215 _____

Needs Work   1   2   3   4   5   Excellent
Paid attention to punctuation

Needs Work   1   2   3   4   5   Excellent
Sounded good

Total Words Read _____

Total Errors − _____

Correct WPM _____

Hawaiian Hurricane

	Words Read	Miscues

On September 11, 1993, Hurricane Iniki, which had been | 9 | _____
moving along a harmless path, took a sharp turn, headed north, | 20 | _____
and made its way straight for Hawaii. Gaining strength as it went, | 32 | _____
the storm carried torrential rains and wind gusts up to 180 miles | 44 | _____
per hour. | 46 | _____

The hurricane dealt only a glancing blow to most of the | 57 | _____
Hawaiian islands. But Iniki hit Kauai with its full force. The | 68 | _____
eye of the storm passed right over the island. | 77 | _____

The roofs on thousands of buildings on the island were blown | 88 | _____
away or damaged. Other buildings were completely destroyed. | 96 | _____
The storm flattened fields of sugar cane. It toppled rows of | 107 | _____
hardwood trees. It also created monstrous 20-foot ocean waves. | 116 | _____
These swept cars away. The waves eroded beaches and washed | 126 | _____
out coastal roads. Boats anchored at Port Allen Harbor were | 136 | _____
piled up on top of each other. | 143 | _____

Iniki also threatened tourists trapped on the island. The | 152 | _____
hurricane blasted their hotels. Guests were forced to flee inland | 162 | _____
and wait in long lines at grocery stores to buy food and water. The | 176 | _____
damage to Kauai's luxury hotels was so extensive that nine months | 187 | _____
after the hurricane only four of the 11 hotels had reopened. | 198 | _____

The governor of Hawaii said it was probably the worst disaster | 209 | _____
in the history of the state. | 215 | _____

Needs Work   1 2 3 4 5   Excellent
Paid attention to punctuation

Needs Work   1 2 3 4 5   Excellent
Sounded good

Total Words Read _____

Total Errors − _____

Correct WPM _____

54

Nonfiction

from *Babe Didrikson Zaharias:*
The Making of a Champion
by Russell Freedman

First Reading

	Words Read	Miscues

⸎⸎⸎

During the day-long contest, the lead shifted back and forth.	10	_____
At the twelfth hole, Babe led by five points. But Chandler	21	_____
closed the gap and by the twenty-fourth hole was three up	32	_____
(three points ahead). Didrikson rallied and evened the score	41	_____
on the thirty-third hole.	45	_____
Suspense mounted as the gallery followed the golfers to the	55	_____
thirty-fourth hole. Chandler reached the green on her third shot;	65	_____
the ball was within two feet of the cup, and she seemed certain	78	_____
to take the hole in four.	84	_____
Babe's first shot, a powerful 250-yard drive, had landed in a	95	_____
ditch. Her second shot skidded across the green, rolled onto a	106	_____
roadway used by trucks, and dropped into a wheel rut holding a	118	_____
puddle of rainwater from the day before. The top of the ball was	131	_____
just visible above the water.	136	_____
Babe studied her third shot carefully, then took a sand wedge	147	_____
and swung. With a splash of mud and water, the ball leaped out	160	_____
of the rut, bounced across the green, and rolled into the hole! The	173	_____
gallery burst into whistles, cheers, and applause. Dozens of people	183	_____
rushed forward to congratulate Babe, and in the excitement, she	193	_____
was knocked facedown into the mud.	199	_____

Needs Work 1 2 3 4 5 Excellent
Paid attention to punctuation

Needs Work 1 2 3 4 5 Excellent
Sounded good

Total Words Read _____

Total Errors − _____

Correct WPM _____

from *Babe Didrikson Zaharias:*

The Making of a Champion

by Russell Freedman

	Words Read	Miscues

During the day-long contest, the lead shifted back and forth.   10 _____

At the twelfth hole, Babe led by five points. But Chandler   21 _____

closed the gap and by the twenty-fourth hole was three up   32 _____

(three points ahead). Didrikson rallied and evened the score   41 _____

on the thirty-third hole.   45 _____

Suspense mounted as the gallery followed the golfers to the   55 _____

thirty-fourth hole. Chandler reached the green on her third shot;   65 _____

the ball was within two feet of the cup, and she seemed certain   78 _____

to take the hole in four.   84 _____

Babe's first shot, a powerful 250-yard drive, had landed in a   95 _____

ditch. Her second shot skidded across the green, rolled onto a   106 _____

roadway used by trucks, and dropped into a wheel rut holding a   118 _____

puddle of rainwater from the day before. The top of the ball was   131 _____

just visible above the water.   136 _____

Babe studied her third shot carefully, then took a sand wedge   147 _____

and swung. With a splash of mud and water, the ball leaped out   160 _____

of the rut, bounced across the green, and rolled into the hole! The   173 _____

gallery burst into whistles, cheers, and applause. Dozens of people   183 _____

rushed forward to congratulate Babe, and in the excitement, she   193 _____

was knocked facedown into the mud.   199 _____

Needs Work   1   2   3   4   5   Excellent
  Paid attention to punctuation

Needs Work   1   2   3   4   5   Excellent
  Sounded good

Total Words Read _____

Total Errors − _____

Correct WPM _____

55

Fiction

from *Cress Delahanty*
by Jessamyn West

First Reading

	Words Read	Miscues

~~~~~~~~~~

	Words Read	Miscues
She stood warming herself, happy and bemused, like a	9	_____
prisoner unexpectedly pardoned. Then she heard again the click,	18	_____
click she had not recognized. Brownie at the back door!	28	_____
"Oh, poor Brownie, I forgot you. Poor kitty, are you hungry?"	39	_____
There was Brownie sitting on the back step, with fur blown and	51	_____
dusty, patiently waiting to be let in and fed. She was a young	64	_____
cat, who had never had a kit of her own, but she looked like a	79	_____
grandmother. She looked as if she should have a gingham apron	90	_____
tied around her waist, and spectacles on her nose, and now out	102	_____
of her grandmother's eyes she gave Cress a look of tolerance.	113	_____
Cress snatched the cat up and held her close to her face, and	126	_____
rubbed her nose in the soft, cool fur. When she got out the can	140	_____
of evaporated milk she set Brownie by the fire and poured the	152	_____
milk into the bowl from which she had eaten her own lunch.	164	_____
Brownie lapped the yellow arc as it fell from can to bowl.	176	_____
Cress crouched on the hearth with her eyes almost on a level	188	_____
with Brownie's. It was blissful, almost mesmeric to watch the	198	_____
quick, deft dart of the red tongue into the yellow milk.	209	_____

Needs Work   1   2   3   4   5   Excellent
Paid attention to punctuation

Needs Work   1   2   3   4   5   Excellent
Sounded good

Total Words Read   _____

Total Errors   − _____

Correct WPM   _____

from *Cress Delahanty*

by Jessamyn West

	Words Read	Miscues
She stood warming herself, happy and bemused, like a	9	_____
prisoner unexpectedly pardoned. Then she heard again the click,	18	_____
click she had not recognized. Brownie at the back door!	28	_____
"Oh, poor Brownie, I forgot you. Poor kitty, are you hungry?"	39	_____
There was Brownie sitting on the back step, with fur blown and	51	_____
dusty, patiently waiting to be let in and fed. She was a young	64	_____
cat, who had never had a kit of her own, but she looked like a	79	_____
grandmother. She looked as if she should have a gingham apron	90	_____
tied around her waist, and spectacles on her nose, and now out	102	_____
of her grandmother's eyes she gave Cress a look of tolerance.	113	_____
Cress snatched the cat up and held her close to her face, and	126	_____
rubbed her nose in the soft, cool fur. When she got out the can	140	_____
of evaporated milk she set Brownie by the fire and poured the	152	_____
milk into the bowl from which she had eaten her own lunch.	164	_____
Brownie lapped the yellow arc as it fell from can to bowl.	176	_____
Cress crouched on the hearth with her eyes almost on a level	188	_____
with Brownie's. It was blissful, almost mesmeric to watch the	198	_____
quick, deft dart of the red tongue into the yellow milk.	209	_____

Needs Work   1   2   3   4   5   Excellent
Paid attention to punctuation

Needs Work   1   2   3   4   5   Excellent
Sounded good

Total Words Read   _____

Total Errors   − _____

Correct WPM   _____

56

Fiction

from *The Swiss Family Robinson*
by Johann Wyss

First Reading

	Words Read	Miscues

Amid the roar of the thundering waves I suddenly heard the | 11 | _____
cry of "Land, land!" while at the same instant the ship struck with | 24 | _____
a frightful shock, which threw everyone to the deck, and seemed | 35 | _____
to threaten her immediate destruction. | 40 | _____

Dreadful sounds betokened the breaking up of the ship, and | 50 | _____
the roaring waters poured in on all sides. | 58 | _____

Then the voice of the captain was heard above the tumult, | 69 | _____
shouting, "Lower away the boats! We are lost!" | 77 | _____

"Lost!" I exclaimed, and the word went like a dagger to my | 89 | _____
heart; but seeing my children's terror renewed, I composed myself, | 99 | _____
calling out cheerfully, "Take courage, my boys! We are all above | 110 | _____
water yet. There is the land not far off; let us do our best to reach | 126 | _____
it. You know God helps those that help themselves!" With that, I | 138 | _____
left them and went on deck. What was my horror when through | 150 | _____
the foam and spray I beheld the only remaining boat leave the | 162 | _____
ship, the last of the seamen spring into her and push off, regardless | 175 | _____
of my cries and entreaties that we might be allowed to share their | 188 | _____
slender chance of preserving their lives. My voice was drowned in | 199 | _____
the howling of the blast; and even had the crew wished it, the | 212 | _____
return of the boat was impossible. | 218 | _____

Needs Work   1 2 3 4 5   Excellent
Paid attention to punctuation

Needs Work   1 2 3 4 5   Excellent
Sounded good

Total Words Read _____

Total Errors – _____

Correct WPM _____

56

Fiction

from *The Swiss Family Robinson*
by Johann Wyss

Second Reading

	Words Read	Miscues

Amid the roar of the thundering waves I suddenly heard the | 11 | _____
cry of "Land, land!" while at the same instant the ship struck with | 24 | _____
a frightful shock, which threw everyone to the deck, and seemed | 35 | _____
to threaten her immediate destruction. | 40 | _____

Dreadful sounds betokened the breaking up of the ship, and | 50 | _____
the roaring waters poured in on all sides. | 58 | _____

Then the voice of the captain was heard above the tumult, | 69 | _____
shouting, "Lower away the boats! We are lost!" | 77 | _____

"Lost!" I exclaimed, and the word went like a dagger to my | 89 | _____
heart; but seeing my children's terror renewed, I composed myself, | 99 | _____
calling out cheerfully, "Take courage, my boys! We are all above | 110 | _____
water yet. There is the land not far off; let us do our best to reach | 126 | _____
it. You know God helps those that help themselves!" With that, I | 138 | _____
left them and went on deck. What was my horror when through | 150 | _____
the foam and spray I beheld the only remaining boat leave the | 162 | _____
ship, the last of the seamen spring into her and push off, regardless | 175 | _____
of my cries and entreaties that we might be allowed to share their | 188 | _____
slender chance of preserving their lives. My voice was drowned in | 199 | _____
the howling of the blast; and even had the crew wished it, the | 212 | _____
return of the boat was impossible. | 218 | _____

Needs Work   1 2 3 4 5   Excellent
Paid attention to punctuation

Needs Work   1 2 3 4 5   Excellent
Sounded good

Total Words Read _____

Total Errors − _____

Correct WPM _____

57
Nonfiction

The Great San Francisco Earthquake

First Reading

	Words Read	Miscues

The evening of October 17, 1989, was warm and breezy. ⟨10⟩

"Good earthquake weather," Sara Kidd thought as she left her ⟨20⟩

San Francisco office. Moments later, the building began to shake. ⟨30⟩

Sara watched in horror as the double-decker highway across the ⟨40⟩

street collapsed onto the lower roadway, flattening cars like tin ⟨50⟩

cans. All around, buildings swayed and crumpled. Roads bulged ⟨59⟩

and rippled, bouncing cars around like an amusement park ride. ⟨69⟩

This was no ride, though. It was the third most lethal earthquake ⟨81⟩

in U.S. history. ⟨84⟩

As suddenly as it started, the shaking stopped. Sara ⟨93⟩

remembered her grandfather's stories about the great San ⟨101⟩

Francisco earthquake of 1906. He had been awakened by a ⟨111⟩

howling noise, he said. The earth rumbled, shook, and pitched. ⟨121⟩

He ran into the street just before his house fell apart, reduced ⟨133⟩

to kindling. Fueled by overturned stoves, scattered blazes joined ⟨142⟩

together into firestorms that roared across the city. By the time ⟨153⟩

the fires died out three days later, 28,188 buildings had been ⟨164⟩

destroyed, and 2,500 people had died. ⟨170⟩

The city had learned its lesson from the quake of '06: Be ⟨182⟩

prepared! Although the quake of '89 was costly, only about 100 ⟨193⟩

people died. "I'm happy this wasn't 'The Big One,'" Sara said. ⟨204⟩

Needs Work   1   2   3   4   5   Excellent
Paid attention to punctuation

Needs Work   1   2   3   4   5   Excellent
Sounded good

Total Words Read _____

Total Errors − _____

Correct WPM _____

113

The Great San Francisco Earthquake

	Words Read	Miscues

The evening of October 17, 1989, was warm and breezy. | 10 | _____

"Good earthquake weather," Sara Kidd thought as she left her | 20 | _____

San Francisco office. Moments later, the building began to shake. | 30 | _____

Sara watched in horror as the double-decker highway across the | 40 | _____

street collapsed onto the lower roadway, flattening cars like tin | 50 | _____

cans. All around, buildings swayed and crumpled. Roads bulged | 59 | _____

and rippled, bouncing cars around like an amusement park ride. | 69 | _____

This was no ride, though. It was the third most lethal earthquake | 81 | _____

in U.S. history. | 84 | _____

As suddenly as it started, the shaking stopped. Sara | 93 | _____

remembered her grandfather's stories about the great San | 101 | _____

Francisco earthquake of 1906. He had been awakened by a | 111 | _____

howling noise, he said. The earth rumbled, shook, and pitched. | 121 | _____

He ran into the street just before his house fell apart, reduced | 133 | _____

to kindling. Fueled by overturned stoves, scattered blazes joined | 142 | _____

together into firestorms that roared across the city. By the time | 153 | _____

the fires died out three days later, 28,188 buildings had been | 164 | _____

destroyed, and 2,500 people had died. | 170 | _____

The city had learned its lesson from the quake of '06: Be | 182 | _____

prepared! Although the quake of '89 was costly, only about 100 | 193 | _____

people died. "I'm happy this wasn't 'The Big One,'" Sara said. | 204 | _____

Needs Work   1   2   3   4   5   Excellent
Paid attention to punctuation

Needs Work   1   2   3   4   5   Excellent
Sounded good

Total Words Read   _____

Total Errors   − _____

Correct WPM   _____

58 from "The Force of Luck"

retold by Rudolfo A. Anaya

Fiction

First Reading

	Words Read	Miscues

⟨⟨⟨⟨⟨⟩⟩⟩⟩⟩

	Words Read	Miscues
Once two wealthy friends got into a heated argument. One	10	_____
said that it was money which made a man prosperous, and the	22	_____
other maintained that it wasn't money, but luck, which made the	33	_____
man. They argued for some time and finally decided that if only	45	_____
they could find an honorable man then perhaps they could prove	56	_____
their respective points of view.	61	_____
One day while they were passing through a small village they	72	_____
came upon a miller who was grinding corn and wheat. They paused	84	_____
to ask the man how he ran his business. The miller replied that he	98	_____
worked for a master and that he earned only four bits a day, and	112	_____
with that he had to support a family of five.	122	_____
The friends were surprised. "Do you mean to tell us you can	134	_____
maintain a family of five on only fifteen dollars a month?" one asked.	147	_____
"I live modestly to make ends meet," the humble miller replied.	158	_____
The two friends privately agreed that if they put this man to a	171	_____
test perhaps they could resolve their argument.	178	_____
"I am going to make you an offer," one of them said to the	192	_____
miller. "I will give you two hundred dollars and you may do	204	_____
whatever you want with the money."	210	_____

Needs Work   1 2 3 4 5   Excellent
Paid attention to punctuation

Needs Work   1 2 3 4 5   Excellent
Sounded good

Total Words Read _____

Total Errors – _____

Correct WPM _____

from "The Force of Luck"

retold by Rudolfo A. Anaya

	Words Read	Miscues

Once two wealthy friends got into a heated argument. One said that it was money which made a man prosperous, and the other maintained that it wasn't money, but luck, which made the man. They argued for some time and finally decided that if only they could find an honorable man then perhaps they could prove their respective points of view.

One day while they were passing through a small village they came upon a miller who was grinding corn and wheat. They paused to ask the man how he ran his business. The miller replied that he worked for a master and that he earned only four bits a day, and with that he had to support a family of five.

The friends were surprised. "Do you mean to tell us you can maintain a family of five on only fifteen dollars a month?" one asked.

"I live modestly to make ends meet," the humble miller replied.

The two friends privately agreed that if they put this man to a test perhaps they could resolve their argument.

"I am going to make you an offer," one of them said to the miller. "I will give you two hundred dollars and you may do whatever you want with the money."

Words Read
10
22
33
45
56
61
72
84
98
112
122
134
147
158
171
178
192
204
210

Needs Work   1   2   3   4   5   Excellent
Paid attention to punctuation

Needs Work   1   2   3   4   5   Excellent
Sounded good

Total Words Read _____

Total Errors − _____

Correct WPM _____

59

Nonfiction

The Eddystone Lighthouse

	Words Read	Miscues

As long as people have loved adventure, they have braved the   11   _____

open seas. With only small, fragile boats to protect them, mariners   22   _____

of long ago set out to explore and to trade. And ever since mariners   36   _____

began traveling across oceans and lakes, they have faced danger.   46   _____

But if they were lucky, before trouble hit they would see the   58   _____

welcome beam of a lighthouse. Its light would guide them home.   69   _____

Early lighthouses were all built on land. Even though ships   79   _____

often ran into trouble on offshore rocks, people thought it was   90   _____

impossible to build a lighthouse near a dangerous area. In 1965   101   _____

a talented builder named Harry Winstanley took on the task of   112   _____

building an offshore lighthouse. He chose a spot where many   122   _____

shipwrecks had taken place—the Eddystone rocks in England.   131   _____

Building the lighthouse took years. Only when the weather   140   _____

was good could the crew row the 14 miles to the building site.   153   _____

On bad days, waves would wash over the site and sometimes   164   _____

undo what had been done the day before. When the lighthouse   175   _____

finally opened, it became a tourist attraction. Winstanley's   183   _____

Eddystone light operated for only five years before it was   193   _____

destroyed by a huge storm. A second and then a third light were   206   _____

built; each was destroyed. Today a fourth Eddystone light stands   216   _____

on the site.   219   _____

Needs Work   1   2   3   4   5   Excellent

Paid attention to punctuation

Needs Work   1   2   3   4   5   Excellent

Sounded good

Total Words Read _____

Total Errors – _____

Correct WPM _____

The Eddystone Lighthouse

	Words Read	Miscues

As long as people have loved adventure, they have braved the | 11 | _____

open seas. With only small, fragile boats to protect them, mariners | 22 | _____

of long ago set out to explore and to trade. And ever since mariners | 36 | _____

began traveling across oceans and lakes, they have faced danger. | 46 | _____

But if they were lucky, before trouble hit they would see the | 58 | _____

welcome beam of a lighthouse. Its light would guide them home. | 69 | _____

Early lighthouses were all built on land. Even though ships | 79 | _____

often ran into trouble on offshore rocks, people thought it was | 90 | _____

impossible to build a lighthouse near a dangerous area. In 1965 | 101 | _____

a talented builder named Harry Winstanley took on the task of | 112 | _____

building an offshore lighthouse. He chose a spot where many | 122 | _____

shipwrecks had taken place—the Eddystone rocks in England. | 131 | _____

Building the lighthouse took years. Only when the weather | 140 | _____

was good could the crew row the 14 miles to the building site. | 153 | _____

On bad days, waves would wash over the site and sometimes | 164 | _____

undo what had been done the day before. When the lighthouse | 175 | _____

finally opened, it became a tourist attraction. Winstanley's | 183 | _____

Eddystone light operated for only five years before it was | 193 | _____

destroyed by a huge storm. A second and then a third light were | 206 | _____

built; each was destroyed. Today a fourth Eddystone light stands | 216 | _____

on the site. | 219 | _____

Needs Work   1   2   3   4   5   Excellent
Paid attention to punctuation

Needs Work   1   2   3   4   5   Excellent
Sounded good

Total Words Read _____

Total Errors − _____

Correct WPM _____

60

Fiction

from "With All Flags Flying"
by Anne Tyler

First Reading

	Words Read	Miscues

The light changed, the motor roared. Now that they were in | 11 | _____

traffic, he felt more conspicuous, but not in a bad way. People in | 24 | _____

their automobiles seemed sealed in, overprotected; men in large | 33 | _____

trucks must envy the way the motorcycle looped in and out, | 44 | _____

hornet-like, stripped to the bare essentials of a motor and two | 55 | _____

wheels. By tugs at the boy's shirt and single words shouted into | 67 | _____

the wind he directed him to his daughter's house, but he was | 79 | _____

sorry to have the ride over so quickly. | 87 | _____

His daughter had married a salesman and lived in a plain, | 98 | _____

square stone house that the old man approved of. There were | 109 | _____

sneakers and a football in the front yard, signs of a large, happy | 122 | _____

family. A bicycle lay in the driveway. The motorcycle stopped just | 133 | _____

inches from it. "Here we are," the boy said. | 142 | _____

"Well, I surely do thank you." | 148 | _____

He climbed off, fearing for one second that his legs would give | 160 | _____

way beneath him and spoil everything that had gone before. But | 171 | _____

no, they held steady. He took off the helmet and handed it to the | 185 | _____

boy, who waved and roared off. It was a really magnificent roar, | 197 | _____

ear-dazzling. | 198 | _____

Needs Work 1 2 3 4 5 Excellent
Paid attention to punctuation

Needs Work 1 2 3 4 5 Excellent
Sounded good

Total Words Read _____

Total Errors − _____

Correct WPM _____

from "With All Flags Flying"

by Anne Tyler

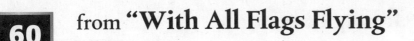

	Words Read	Miscues

The light changed, the motor roared. Now that they were in | 11 | _____
traffic, he felt more conspicuous, but not in a bad way. People in | 24 | _____
their automobiles seemed sealed in, overprotected; men in large | 33 | _____
trucks must envy the way the motorcycle looped in and out, | 44 | _____
hornet-like, stripped to the bare essentials of a motor and two | 55 | _____
wheels. By tugs at the boy's shirt and single words shouted into | 67 | _____
the wind he directed him to his daughter's house, but he was | 79 | _____
sorry to have the ride over so quickly. | 87 | _____

His daughter had married a salesman and lived in a plain, | 98 | _____
square stone house that the old man approved of. There were | 109 | _____
sneakers and a football in the front yard, signs of a large, happy | 122 | _____
family. A bicycle lay in the driveway. The motorcycle stopped just | 133 | _____
inches from it. "Here we are," the boy said. | 142 | _____

"Well, I surely do thank you." | 148 | _____

He climbed off, fearing for one second that his legs would give | 160 | _____
way beneath him and spoil everything that had gone before. But | 171 | _____
no, they held steady. He took off the helmet and handed it to the | 185 | _____
boy, who waved and roared off. It was a really magnificent roar, | 197 | _____
ear-dazzling. | 198 | _____

Needs Work   1   2   3   4   5   Excellent
Paid attention to punctuation

Needs Work   1   2   3   4   5   Excellent
Sounded good

Total Words Read _____

Total Errors − _____

Correct WPM _____

A Silent Army of Clay

Nonfiction

	Words Read	Miscues

⚬⚬⚬

The year was 1974. It was an ordinary day in the Chinese   12 _____
countryside. Farmers were hard at work digging a new well.   22 _____
One digger was surprised when his shovel hit a piece of hard   34 _____
clay. When he pulled out the clay piece, he discovered that it   46 _____
was the head of a statue. More digging revealed the rest of the   59 _____
life-sized statue of an ancient Chinese warrior dressed for battle.   69 _____
The farmers did not find the water they were looking for. Instead   81 _____
they discovered what is thought to be one of the most important   93 _____
finds of the 20th century.   98 _____

The farmers were eager to share their find, so they reported it   110 _____
to local authorities. Excited scientists came to the site and started   121 _____
digging. They knew that the site was close to the ancient tomb   133 _____
of the first emperor of China. Was this statue the only one of its   147 _____
kind, or were there more like it? Could this statue be connected   159 _____
in some way to the emperor's tomb? The answers soon became   170 _____
clear as statue after statue was uncovered. Experts decided that   180 _____
the statues were part of a silent army put in place to defend the   194 _____
emperor after his death. Incredibly, nearly 7,500 clay soldiers   203 _____
dressed for battle have been uncovered.   209 _____

Needs Work   1   2   3   4   5   Excellent
Paid attention to punctuation

Needs Work   1   2   3   4   5   Excellent
Sounded good

Total Words Read _____

Total Errors − _____

Correct WPM _____

A Silent Army of Clay

	Words Read	Miscues
The year was 1974. It was an ordinary day in the Chinese	12	_____
countryside. Farmers were hard at work digging a new well.	22	_____
One digger was surprised when his shovel hit a piece of hard	34	_____
clay. When he pulled out the clay piece, he discovered that it	46	_____
was the head of a statue. More digging revealed the rest of the	59	_____
life-sized statue of an ancient Chinese warrior dressed for battle.	69	_____
The farmers did not find the water they were looking for. Instead	81	_____
they discovered what is thought to be one of the most important	93	_____
finds of the 20th century.	98	_____
The farmers were eager to share their find, so they reported it	110	_____
to local authorities. Excited scientists came to the site and started	121	_____
digging. They knew that the site was close to the ancient tomb	133	_____
of the first emperor of China. Was this statue the only one of its	147	_____
kind, or were there more like it? Could this statue be connected	159	_____
in some way to the emperor's tomb? The answers soon became	170	_____
clear as statue after statue was uncovered. Experts decided that	180	_____
the statues were part of a silent army put in place to defend the	194	_____
emperor after his death. Incredibly, nearly 7,500 clay soldiers	203	_____
dressed for battle have been uncovered.	209	_____

Needs Work 1 2 3 4 5 Excellent
Paid attention to punctuation

Needs Work 1 2 3 4 5 Excellent
Sounded good

Total Words Read _____

Total Errors − _____

Correct WPM _____

62 from "Sucker"
by Carson McCullers

Fiction

	Words Read	Miscues

Whenever I would bring any of my friends back to my room   12   _____

all I had to do was just glance once at Sucker and he would get   27   _____

up from whatever he was busy with and maybe half smile at me,   40   _____

and leave without saying a word. He never brought kids back   51   _____

there. He's twelve, four years younger than I am, and he always   63   _____

knew without me even telling him that I didn't want kids that   75   _____

age meddling with my things.   80   _____

Half the time I used to forget that Sucker isn't my brother. He's   93   _____

my first cousin but practically ever since I remember he's been in   105   _____

our family. You see his folks were killed in a wreck when he was   119   _____

a baby. To me and my kid sisters he was like our brother.   132   _____

Sucker used to always remember and believe every word I   142   _____

said. That's how he got his nick-name. Once a couple of years ago   155   _____

I told him that if he'd jump off our garage with an umbrella it   169   _____

would act as a parachute and he wouldn't fall hard. He did it and   183   _____

busted his knee. That's just one instance. And the funny thing was   195   _____

that no matter how many times he got fooled he would still   207   _____

believe me.   209   _____

Needs Work   1   2   3   4   5   Excellent
Paid attention to punctuation

Needs Work   1   2   3   4   5   Excellent
Sounded good

Total Words Read   _____

Total Errors   – _____

Correct WPM   _____

62

Fiction

from "Sucker"
by Carson McCullers

Second Reading

	Words Read	Miscues

Whenever I would bring any of my friends back to my room | 12 | _____

all I had to do was just glance once at Sucker and he would get | 27 | _____

up from whatever he was busy with and maybe half smile at me, | 40 | _____

and leave without saying a word. He never brought kids back | 51 | _____

there. He's twelve, four years younger than I am, and he always | 63 | _____

knew without me even telling him that I didn't want kids that | 75 | _____

age meddling with my things. | 80 | _____

Half the time I used to forget that Sucker isn't my brother. He's | 93 | _____

my first cousin but practically ever since I remember he's been in | 105 | _____

our family. You see his folks were killed in a wreck when he was | 119 | _____

a baby. To me and my kid sisters he was like our brother. | 132 | _____

Sucker used to always remember and believe every word I | 142 | _____

said. That's how he got his nick-name. Once a couple of years ago | 155 | _____

I told him that if he'd jump off our garage with an umbrella it | 169 | _____

would act as a parachute and he wouldn't fall hard. He did it and | 183 | _____

busted his knee. That's just one instance. And the funny thing was | 195 | _____

that no matter how many times he got fooled he would still | 207 | _____

believe me. | 209 | _____

Needs Work   1 2 3 4 5   Excellent
Paid attention to punctuation

Needs Work   1 2 3 4 5   Excellent
Sounded good

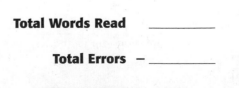

Total Words Read _____

Total Errors – _____

Correct WPM _____

124

from *The Red Pony*
by John Steinbeck

63

Fiction

First Reading

	Words Read	Miscues

Time dragged on toward Thanksgiving, but winter came fast. 9 _____

The clouds swept down and hung all day over the land and 21 _____

brushed the hilltops, and the winds blew shrilly at night. All day 33 _____

the dry oak leaves drifted down from the trees until they covered 45 _____

the ground, and yet the trees were unchanged. 53 _____

Jody had wished it might not rain before Thanksgiving, but 63 _____

it did. The brown earth turned dark and the trees glistened. The 75 _____

cut ends of the [field] stubble turned black with mildew; the 86 _____

haystacks grayed from exposure to the damp, and on the roofs 97 _____

the moss, which had been all summer as gray as lizards, turned a 110 _____

brilliant yellow-green. During the week of rain, Jody kept the pony 121 _____

in the box stall out of the dampness, except for a little time after 135 _____

school when he took him out for exercise and to drink at the 148 _____

water-trough in the upper corral. Not once did Gabilan get wet. 159 _____

The wet weather continued until little new grass appeared. 168 _____

Jody walked to school dressed in a slicker and short rubber boots. 180 _____

At length one morning the sun came out brightly. Jody, at his 192 _____

work in the box stall, said to Billy Buck, "Maybe I'll leave Gabilan 205 _____

in the corral when I go to school today." 214 _____

"Be good for him to be out in the sun," Billy assured him. 227 _____

Needs Work   1   2   3   4   5   Excellent
Paid attention to punctuation

Needs Work   1   2   3   4   5   Excellent
Sounded good

Total Words Read _____

Total Errors − _____

Correct WPM _____

63

Fiction

from *The Red Pony*
by John Steinbeck

Time dragged on toward Thanksgiving, but winter came fast.	9
The clouds swept down and hung all day over the land and	21
brushed the hilltops, and the winds blew shrilly at night. All day	33
the dry oak leaves drifted down from the trees until they covered	45
the ground, and yet the trees were unchanged.	53
Jody had wished it might not rain before Thanksgiving, but	63
it did. The brown earth turned dark and the trees glistened. The	75
cut ends of the [field] stubble turned black with mildew; the	86
haystacks grayed from exposure to the damp, and on the roofs	97
the moss, which had been all summer as gray as lizards, turned a	110
brilliant yellow-green. During the week of rain, Jody kept the pony	121
in the box stall out of the dampness, except for a little time after	135
school when he took him out for exercise and to drink at the	148
water-trough in the upper corral. Not once did Gabilan get wet.	159
The wet weather continued until little new grass appeared.	168
Jody walked to school dressed in a slicker and short rubber boots.	180
At length one morning the sun came out brightly. Jody, at his	192
work in the box stall, said to Billy Buck, "Maybe I'll leave Gabilan	205
in the corral when I go to school today."	214
"Be good for him to be out in the sun," Billy assured him.	227

Needs Work   1 2 3 4 5   Excellent
Paid attention to punctuation

Needs Work   1 2 3 4 5   Excellent
Sounded good

Total Words Read _____

Total Errors − _____

Correct WPM _____

126

64

Nonfiction

from "Jane Addams"
by William Jay Jacobs

First Reading

	Words Read	Miscues

⟨❈❈❈⟩

It was hard for people living on Halsted Street to remember | 11 | _____

the beauty of nature. All around them they saw concrete and | 22 | _____

ugliness. So Jane Addams arranged for the children to go to | 33 | _____

camps along Lake Michigan. She also planned trips to the country | 44 | _____

for the adults. Some of the adults did not know there were lovely | 57 | _____

places in America. They thought the whole nation was like the | 68 | _____

streets of Chicago. | 71 | _____

As the newspapers began to write about Hull House, many | 81 | _____

wealthy young women were drawn there. Like Jane Addams | 90 | _____

and Ellen Starr, they wanted to do their share in making a better | 103 | _____

world. And they had the education and free time to do something | 115 | _____

about it. | 117 | _____

With more helpers the activities of Hull House grew. There | 127 | _____

was a playground for children—the first one in Chicago—so that | 139 | _____

youngsters would not have to play in the streets. There were clubs | 151 | _____

and classes for young people who had to work and could not go | 164 | _____

to high school. There was a music school. There was a nursery | 176 | _____

where working mothers could leave their children during the | 185 | _____

day. People were asked to pay a small amount of money for these | 198 | _____

services so they would not feel they were taking charity. | 208 | _____

Needs Work   1   2   3   4   5   Excellent
Paid attention to punctuation

Needs Work   1   2   3   4   5   Excellent
Sounded good

Total Words Read _____

Total Errors − _____

Correct WPM _____

from "Jane Addams"
by William Jay Jacobs

Second Reading

	Words Read	Miscues

It was hard for people living on Halsted Street to remember | 11 | _____

the beauty of nature. All around them they saw concrete and | 22 | _____

ugliness. So Jane Addams arranged for the children to go to | 33 | _____

camps along Lake Michigan. She also planned trips to the country | 44 | _____

for the adults. Some of the adults did not know there were lovely | 57 | _____

places in America. They thought the whole nation was like the | 68 | _____

streets of Chicago. | 71 | _____

As the newspapers began to write about Hull House, many | 81 | _____

wealthy young women were drawn there. Like Jane Addams | 90 | _____

and Ellen Starr, they wanted to do their share in making a better | 103 | _____

world. And they had the education and free time to do something | 115 | _____

about it. | 117 | _____

With more helpers the activities of Hull House grew. There | 127 | _____

was a playground for children—the first one in Chicago—so that | 139 | _____

youngsters would not have to play in the streets. There were clubs | 151 | _____

and classes for young people who had to work and could not go | 164 | _____

to high school. There was a music school. There was a nursery | 176 | _____

where working mothers could leave their children during the | 185 | _____

day. People were asked to pay a small amount of money for these | 198 | _____

services so they would not feel they were taking charity. | 208 | _____

Needs Work   1   2   3   4   5   Excellent
Paid attention to punctuation

Needs Work   1   2   3   4   5   Excellent
Sounded good

Total Words Read _____

Total Errors − _____

Correct WPM _____

65
Nonfiction

The Sky Is Falling!

	Words Read	Miscues

It was September 3, 1970, in the small town of Coffeyville, · 11

Kansas. As the day progressed, clouds began gathering in the · 21

sky. A storm had been forecast. Soon darker clouds appeared. · 31

The townspeople watched the approaching thunderstorm. It · 38

was a hailstorm! · 41

The ice pellets bounced when they hit the pavement. The · 51

hail clattered over the roofs of cars and buildings. People moved · 62

indoors to wait out the storm. Some hailstones were so large it · 74

was frightening. One hailstone measured $17\frac{1}{2}$ inches in · 82

circumference and $5\frac{1}{2}$ inches in diameter. It weighed $1\frac{2}{3}$ · 91

pounds! This was the largest hailstone ever recorded in the · 101

United States. · 103

It would have taken an extremely strong updraft to toss · 113

the hailstone repeatedly up into the top of a cloud and form a · 126

hailstone the size of a football. When people in Coffeyville cut · 137

the hailstone in half, they could see many separate layers of ice. · 149

Fortunately this hailstone did not injure anyone. Hailstones · 157

have killed only two people in the United States. However, · 167

hailstones can cause damage to people, livestock, and property. · 176

If you find yourself caught in a hailstorm, find shelter as quickly · 188

as possible. Watch the storm from the safety of your home! · 199

Needs Work   1   2   3   4   5   Excellent
Paid attention to punctuation

Needs Work   1   2   3   4   5   Excellent
Sounded good

Total Words Read _____

Total Errors − _____

Correct WPM _____

The Sky Is Falling!

	Words Read	Miscues

It was September 3, 1970, in the small town of Coffeyville,   11   _____

Kansas. As the day progressed, clouds began gathering in the   21   _____

sky. A storm had been forecast. Soon darker clouds appeared.   31   _____

The townspeople watched the approaching thunderstorm. It   38   _____

was a hailstorm!   41   _____

     The ice pellets bounced when they hit the pavement. The   51   _____

hail clattered over the roofs of cars and buildings. People moved   62   _____

indoors to wait out the storm. Some hailstones were so large it   74   _____

was frightening. One hailstone measured $17\frac{1}{2}$ inches in   82   _____

circumference and $5\frac{1}{2}$ inches in diameter. It weighed $1\frac{2}{3}$ 91   _____

pounds! This was the largest hailstone ever recorded in the   101   _____

United States.   103   _____

     It would have taken an extremely strong updraft to toss   113   _____

the hailstone repeatedly up into the top of a cloud and form a   126   _____

hailstone the size of a football. When people in Coffeyville cut   137   _____

the hailstone in half, they could see many separate layers of ice.   149   _____

     Fortunately this hailstone did not injure anyone. Hailstones   157   _____

have killed only two people in the United States. However,   167   _____

hailstones can cause damage to people, livestock, and property.   176   _____

If you find yourself caught in a hailstorm, find shelter as quickly   188   _____

as possible. Watch the storm from the safety of your home!   199   _____

Needs Work   1   2   3   4   5   Excellent
Paid attention to punctuation

Needs Work   1   2   3   4   5   Excellent
Sounded good

Total Words Read   _____

Total Errors   − _____

Correct WPM   _____

"Uncle Tony's Goat"
66
Fiction

by Leslie Marmon Silko

First Reading

	Words Read	Miscues

όόό

	Words Read	Miscues
I hurried over to the goat pen and swung the tall wire gate open.	14	_____
The does and kids came prancing out. They trotted daintily past	25	_____
the pigpen and scattered out, intent on finding leaves and grass to	37	_____
eat. It wasn't until then I noticed that the billy goat hadn't come	50	_____
out of the little wooden shed inside the goat pen. I stood outside	63	_____
the pen and tried to look inside the wooden shelter, but it was	76	_____
still early and the morning sun left the inside of the shelter in	89	_____
deep shadow. I stood there for a while, hoping that he would	101	_____
come out by himself, but I realized that he'd recognized me and	113	_____
that he wouldn't come out. I understood right away what was	124	_____
happening and my fear of him was in my bowels and down my	137	_____
neck; I was shaking.	141	_____
Finally my uncle came out of the house; it was time for	153	_____
breakfast. "What's wrong?" he called from the door.	161	_____
"The billy goat won't come out," I yelled back, hoping he	172	_____
would look disgusted and come do it himself.	180	_____
"Get in there and get him out," he said as he went back into	194	_____
the house.	196	_____

Needs Work   1   2   3   4   5   Excellent
Paid attention to punctuation

Needs Work   1   2   3   4   5   Excellent
Sounded good

Total Words Read   _____

Total Errors − _____

Correct WPM   _____

"Uncle Tony's Goat"

by Leslie Marmon Silko

	Words Read	Miscues
I hurried over to the goat pen and swung the tall wire gate open.	14	_____
The does and kids came prancing out. They trotted daintily past	25	_____
the pigpen and scattered out, intent on finding leaves and grass to	37	_____
eat. It wasn't until then I noticed that the billy goat hadn't come	50	_____
out of the little wooden shed inside the goat pen. I stood outside	63	_____
the pen and tried to look inside the wooden shelter, but it was	76	_____
still early and the morning sun left the inside of the shelter in	89	_____
deep shadow. I stood there for a while, hoping that he would	101	_____
come out by himself, but I realized that he'd recognized me and	113	_____
that he wouldn't come out. I understood right away what was	124	_____
happening and my fear of him was in my bowels and down my	137	_____
neck; I was shaking.	141	_____
Finally my uncle came out of the house; it was time for	153	_____
breakfast. "What's wrong?" he called from the door.	161	_____
"The billy goat won't come out," I yelled back, hoping he	172	_____
would look disgusted and come do it himself.	180	_____
"Get in there and get him out," he said as he went back into	194	_____
the house.	196	_____

Needs Work   1   2   3   4   5   Excellent
Paid attention to punctuation

Needs Work   1   2   3   4   5   Excellent
Sounded good

Total Words Read _____

Total Errors − _____

Correct WPM _____

67

Nonfiction

from *Milk: The Fight for Purity*
by James Cross Giblin

First Reading

	Words Read	Miscues

Some milk sellers carried their milk supply in buckets — 9

suspended from yokes across their shoulders, like the milkmaids — 18

of London. Others sold their milk from the backs of horse-drawn — 29

wagons. The milk delivered by wagon was usually contained in — 39

large metal cans. Sometimes the cans had lids, sometimes not. — 49

As the seller walked or rode through the streets, he would — 60

often call, "Milk come! Milk come!" Then he might go on to — 72

chant: — 73

"Here's new milk from the cow, — 79

Which is so nice and so fine, — 86

That the doctors do say — 91

It is much better than wine." — 97

When a housewife heard the seller's call, she would come out — 108

into the street with a pitcher or a pail, and the seller would fill it — 123

from one of his cans. He used a quart measure so that he'd know — 137

how much to charge. In the 1830s, milk sold in New York City — 150

and other American cities for four to six cents a quart. — 161

Milk sellers also roamed the streets of London, where they — 171

had replaced the milkmaids of earlier times. Many of their — 181

customers looked on the sellers with suspicion. They claimed — 190

that the men possessed "neither character, nor decency of manner, — 200

nor cleanliness." — 202

Needs Work   1   2   3   4   5   Excellent
Paid attention to punctuation

Needs Work   1   2   3   4   5   Excellent
Sounded good

Total Words Read _____

Total Errors − _____

Correct WPM _____

133

from *Milk: The Fight for Purity*
by James Cross Giblin

Some milk sellers carried their milk supply in buckets	9	_____
suspended from yokes across their shoulders, like the milkmaids	18	_____
of London. Others sold their milk from the backs of horse-drawn	29	_____
wagons. The milk delivered by wagon was usually contained in	39	_____
large metal cans. Sometimes the cans had lids, sometimes not.	49	_____
As the seller walked or rode through the streets, he would	60	_____
often call, "Milk come! Milk come!" Then he might go on to	72	_____
chant:	73	_____
		_____

> *"Here's new milk from the cow,* — 79
>
> *Which is so nice and so fine,* — 86
>
> *That the doctors do say* — 91
>
> *It is much better than wine."* — 97

When a housewife heard the seller's call, she would come out	108	_____
into the street with a pitcher or a pail, and the seller would fill it	123	_____
from one of his cans. He used a quart measure so that he'd know	137	_____
how much to charge. In the 1830s, milk sold in New York City	150	_____
and other American cities for four to six cents a quart.	161	_____
Milk sellers also roamed the streets of London, where they	171	_____
had replaced the milkmaids of earlier times. Many of their	181	_____
customers looked on the sellers with suspicion. They claimed	190	_____
that the men possessed "neither character, nor decency of manner,	200	_____
nor cleanliness."	202	_____

Needs Work   1 2 3 4 5   Excellent
Paid attention to punctuation

Needs Work   1 2 3 4 5   Excellent
Sounded good

Total Words Read _____

Total Errors − _____

Correct WPM _____

68

Fiction

from **"Caught by a Hair-String"**

retold by Donna Rosenberg

	Words Read	Miscues

Deep in the woods, on the outer edge of a large camp of the   14 _____

People, lived an old man and his wife. They had two daughters   26 _____

who were very beautiful but were so shy that they hid from   38 _____

anyone who wished to see them. One suitor after another wished   49 _____

to marry them, but neither daughter would consider any of these   60 _____

young men.   62 _____

Now the chief of the People had a son who wished to   74 _____

marry one of these daughters. So, as was the custom, the chief   86 _____

accompanied his son to the wigwam of the old couple one   97 _____

evening when the sun had gone to its rest. They had a fine time   111 _____

together, eating, playing games, and telling stories. Meanwhile,   119 _____

the maidens hid behind a screen in the wigwam so that they   131 _____

could listen to the chief and his son without being seen by them.   144 _____

When it came time to leave, the chief announced, "My son is   156 _____

a fine hunter. He will be a fine husband. He wishes to marry one   170 _____

of your daughters, and it is time that he had sons of his own."   184 _____

To these words, the maidens' father replied, "Thank you. I will   195 _____

have some word for you when the sun begins its morning journey."   207 _____

Needs Work   1   2   3   4   5   Excellent
Paid attention to punctuation

Needs Work   1   2   3   4   5   Excellent
Sounded good

Total Words Read _____

Total Errors − _____

Correct WPM _____

from "Caught by a Hair-String"

retold by Donna Rosenberg

	Words Read	Miscues

Deep in the woods, on the outer edge of a large camp of the | 14 | _____

People, lived an old man and his wife. They had two daughters | 26 | _____

who were very beautiful but were so shy that they hid from | 38 | _____

anyone who wished to see them. One suitor after another wished | 49 | _____

to marry them, but neither daughter would consider any of these | 60 | _____

young men. | 62 | _____

Now the chief of the People had a son who wished to | 74 | _____

marry one of these daughters. So, as was the custom, the chief | 86 | _____

accompanied his son to the wigwam of the old couple one | 97 | _____

evening when the sun had gone to its rest. They had a fine time | 111 | _____

together, eating, playing games, and telling stories. Meanwhile, | 119 | _____

the maidens hid behind a screen in the wigwam so that they | 131 | _____

could listen to the chief and his son without being seen by them. | 144 | _____

When it came time to leave, the chief announced, "My son is | 156 | _____

a fine hunter. He will be a fine husband. He wishes to marry one | 170 | _____

of your daughters, and it is time that he had sons of his own." | 184 | _____

To these words, the maidens' father replied, "Thank you. I will | 195 | _____

have some word for you when the sun begins its morning journey." | 207 | _____

Needs Work   1   2   3   4   5   Excellent
Paid attention to punctuation

Needs Work   1   2   3   4   5   Excellent
Sounded good

Total Words Read _____

Total Errors − _____

Correct WPM _____

69

Nonfiction

What Is Black Lung?

	Words Read	Miscues

On a frosty morning in the West Virginia mountains, a group | 11 | _____

of men wait at the mouth of a coal mine tunnel that cuts through | 25 | _____

the mountain. They are wearing coveralls and protective helmets | 34 | _____

with cap lamps and are carrying lunch buckets in their hands. | 45 | _____

One miner, however, is adjusting a strange square on his belt. | 56 | _____

It is a small box from which comes a plastic hose that runs up | 70 | _____

to his chest, where it is clipped to his coveralls. | 80 | _____

The device is a dust sampler. A tiny pump in the box sucks | 93 | _____

air continuously through the tube, and a filter traps the dust | 104 | _____

particles. Coal miners used to breathe a lot of dust like this, | 116 | _____

and it gave thousands of them a disease called black lung. | 127 | _____

At the West Virginia mine, the "mantrip" arrives. It is an | 138 | _____

electrically driven car only two feet high. The men climb in, | 149 | _____

lying beneath the protective steel top. After a ten-minute trip, | 159 | _____

they climb out where the coal is cut. A strong breeze ripples their | 172 | _____

clothes. These strong air currents protect them from black lung. | 182 | _____

Large fans create the air currents to capture the coal dust and | 194 | _____

sweep it away from the men. The miner wearing the dust sampler | 206 | _____

moves a cutting machine into place, and the day's work begins. | 217 | _____

Needs Work 1 2 3 4 5 Excellent
Paid attention to punctuation

Needs Work 1 2 3 4 5 Excellent
Sounded good

Total Words Read _____

Total Errors – _____

Correct WPM _____

What Is Black Lung?

	Words Read	Miscues

On a frosty morning in the West Virginia mountains, a group | 11 | _____
of men wait at the mouth of a coal mine tunnel that cuts through | 25 | _____
the mountain. They are wearing coveralls and protective helmets | 34 | _____
with cap lamps and are carrying lunch buckets in their hands. | 45 | _____
One miner, however, is adjusting a strange square on his belt. | 56 | _____
It is a small box from which comes a plastic hose that runs up | 70 | _____
to his chest, where it is clipped to his coveralls. | 80 | _____

The device is a dust sampler. A tiny pump in the box sucks | 93 | _____
air continuously through the tube, and a filter traps the dust | 104 | _____
particles. Coal miners used to breathe a lot of dust like this, | 116 | _____
and it gave thousands of them a disease called black lung. | 127 | _____

At the West Virginia mine, the "mantrip" arrives. It is an | 138 | _____
electrically driven car only two feet high. The men climb in, | 149 | _____
lying beneath the protective steel top. After a ten-minute trip, | 159 | _____
they climb out where the coal is cut. A strong breeze ripples their | 172 | _____
clothes. These strong air currents protect them from black lung. | 182 | _____
Large fans create the air currents to capture the coal dust and | 194 | _____
sweep it away from the men. The miner wearing the dust sampler | 206 | _____
moves a cutting machine into place, and the day's work begins. | 217 | _____

Needs Work   1   2   3   4   5   Excellent
Paid attention to punctuation

Needs Work   1   2   3   4   5   Excellent
Sounded good

Total Words Read _____

Total Errors − _____

Correct WPM _____

70

Nonfiction

from *Woodsong*
by Gary Paulsen

	Words Read	Miscues

We have bear trouble. Because we feed processed meat to | 10 | _____

the dogs there is always the smell of meat over the kennel. In the | 24 | _____

summer it can be a bit high because the dogs like to "save" their | 38 | _____

food sometimes for a day or two or four—burying it to dig up | 52 | _____

later. We live on the edge of wilderness and consequently the | 63 | _____

meat smell brings any number of visitors from the woods. | 73 | _____

Skunks abound, and foxes and coyotes and wolves and weasels— | 83 | _____

all predators. We once had an eagle live over the kennel for more | 96 | _____

than a week, scavenging from the dogs, and a crazy group of | 108 | _____

ravens has pretty much taken over the puppy pen. Ravens are | 119 | _____

protected by the state and they seem to know it. When I walk | 132 | _____

toward the puppy pen with the buckets of meat it's a toss-up to | 145 | _____

see who gets it—the pups or the birds. They have actually pecked | 158 | _____

the puppies away from the food pans until they have gone | 169 | _____

through and taken what they want. | 175 | _____

Spring, when the bears come, is the worst. They have been in | 187 | _____

hibernation through the winter, and they are hungry beyond caution. | 197 | _____

Needs Work   1 2 3 4 5   Excellent
Paid attention to punctuation

Needs Work   1 2 3 4 5   Excellent
Sounded good

Total Words Read _____

Total Errors − _____

Correct WPM _____

from **Woodsong**

by Gary Paulsen

	Words Read	Miscues
We have bear trouble. Because we feed processed meat to	10	_____
the dogs there is always the smell of meat over the kennel. In the	24	_____
summer it can be a bit high because the dogs like to "save" their	38	_____
food sometimes for a day or two or four—burying it to dig up	52	_____
later. We live on the edge of wilderness and consequently the	63	_____
meat smell brings any number of visitors from the woods.	73	_____
Skunks abound, and foxes and coyotes and wolves and weasels—	83	_____
all predators. We once had an eagle live over the kennel for more	96	_____
than a week, scavenging from the dogs, and a crazy group of	108	_____
ravens has pretty much taken over the puppy pen. Ravens are	119	_____
protected by the state and they seem to know it. When I walk	132	_____
toward the puppy pen with the buckets of meat it's a toss-up to	145	_____
see who gets it—the pups or the birds. They have actually pecked	158	_____
the puppies away from the food pans until they have gone	169	_____
through and taken what they want.	175	_____
Spring, when the bears come, is the worst. They have been in	187	_____
hibernation through the winter, and they are hungry beyond caution.	197	_____

Needs Work   1   2   3   4   5   Excellent
Paid attention to punctuation

Needs Work   1   2   3   4   5   Excellent
Sounded good

Total Words Read _____

Total Errors − _____

Correct WPM _____

71
Nonfiction

from *Unconditional Surrender:*
U. S. Grant and the Civil War

by Albert Marrin

First Reading

	Words Read	Miscues

[Ulysses S.] Grant was liked by his [West Point] classmates, — 10 — ____

who admired his horsemanship. Even the half-wild York, demon — 19 — ____

of the stables, calmly went through his paces with Grant in the — 31 — ____

saddle. Moreover, Grant could stand up for himself. Jack Lindsay, — 41 — ____

a colonel's son and the faculty's pet, was the school bully. A big, — 54 — ____

strapping fellow, he thought it great fun to shove Grant, half his — 66 — ____

size, out of the drill line. Grant asked him to stop, but that only — 80 — ____

encouraged him. Then he shoved once too often. Grant spun — 90 — ____

around and, in a flurry of fists, knocked him down. The other — 102 — ____

cadets stood at attention, chins in, chests out, grinning from — 112 — ____

ear to ear. No one, of course, knew what had happened to poor — 125 — ____

Lindsay, and he was too ashamed to tell. — 133 — ____

Grant's classwork left room for improvement. Although he — 141 — ____

excelled in mathematics, in other subjects he studied only enough — 151 — ____

to pass. He took no interest in military affairs. He read none of — 164 — ____

the military classics and knew little more of history's great soldiers — 175 — ____

than their names. Napoleon, for all he cared, could have been the — 187 — ____

inventor of a cream-filled pastry. The French emperor's campaigns, — 196 — ____

which others studied in minute detail, were a mystery to the — 207 — ____

tanner's son. His favorite reading was novels borrowed from the — 217 — ____

academy library. — 219 — ____

Needs Work 1 2 3 4 5 Excellent
Paid attention to punctuation

Needs Work 1 2 3 4 5 Excellent
Sounded good

Total Words Read _____

Total Errors − _____

Correct WPM _____

71

Nonfiction

from *Unconditional Surrender:*
U. S. Grant and the Civil War
by Albert Marrin

	Words Read	Miscues

[Ulysses S.] Grant was liked by his [West Point] classmates, — 10 _____

who admired his horsemanship. Even the half-wild York, demon — 19 _____

of the stables, calmly went through his paces with Grant in the — 31 _____

saddle. Moreover, Grant could stand up for himself. Jack Lindsay, — 41 _____

a colonel's son and the faculty's pet, was the school bully. A big, — 54 _____

strapping fellow, he thought it great fun to shove Grant, half his — 66 _____

size, out of the drill line. Grant asked him to stop, but that only — 80 _____

encouraged him. Then he shoved once too often. Grant spun — 90 _____

around and, in a flurry of fists, knocked him down. The other — 102 _____

cadets stood at attention, chins in, chests out, grinning from — 112 _____

ear to ear. No one, of course, knew what had happened to poor — 125 _____

Lindsay, and he was too ashamed to tell. — 133 _____

Grant's classwork left room for improvement. Although he — 141 _____

excelled in mathematics, in other subjects he studied only enough — 151 _____

to pass. He took no interest in military affairs. He read none of — 164 _____

the military classics and knew little more of history's great soldiers — 175 _____

than their names. Napoleon, for all he cared, could have been the — 187 _____

inventor of a cream-filled pastry. The French emperor's campaigns, — 196 _____

which others studied in minute detail, were a mystery to the — 207 _____

tanner's son. His favorite reading was novels borrowed from the — 217 _____

academy library. — 219 _____

Needs Work   1 2 3 4 5   Excellent
Paid attention to punctuation

Needs Work   1 2 3 4 5   Excellent
Sounded good

Total Words Read _____

Total Errors − _____

Correct WPM _____

Needles That Cure

by Henry and Melissa Billings

Nonfiction

	Words Read	Miscues

Everyone knows that feet are good for walking, running, and   10   _____

kicking a soccer ball. But did you know that your feet can also   23   _____

play a role in curing headaches, stomachaches, and toothaches?   32   _____

Some people say you can get rid of ailments just by having a   45   _____

specialist jab your foot.   49   _____

It sounds crazy at first. But according to the ancient art of   61   _____

acupuncture, it works. A needle stuck into a specific point on   72   _____

the second toe is said to banish headaches. A needle between   83   _____

the second and third toe can get rid of a sore throat. A needle   97   _____

put into the outside of a foot can stimulate vision.   107   _____

Acupuncture began in China more than four thousand years   116   _____

ago. It is based on the belief that there is a natural flow of energy   131   _____

inside each human being. This energy, or life force, is called *qi*   143   _____

(pronounced CHEE). The qi is said to flow along certain pathways   154   _____

in the body. These pathways, called meridians, are like rivers.   164   _____

When they flow freely, you feel strong and healthy. But if one of   177   _____

your meridians gets blocked, the flow of energy is disrupted. Too   188   _____

much qi builds up in one part of your body. By inserting needles   201   _____

in the right spots, specialists can unblock your meridians and get   212   _____

your qi flowing correctly again.   217   _____

Needs Work   1   2   3   4   5   Excellent
Paid attention to punctuation

Needs Work   1   2   3   4   5   Excellent
Sounded good

Total Words Read _____

Total Errors − _____

Correct WPM _____

72

Nonfiction

Needles That Cure
by Henry and Melissa Billings

	Words Read	Miscues

Everyone knows that feet are good for walking, running, and
kicking a soccer ball. But did you know that your feet can also
play a role in curing headaches, stomachaches, and toothaches?
Some people say you can get rid of ailments just by having a
specialist jab your foot.

It sounds crazy at first. But according to the ancient art of
acupuncture, it works. A needle stuck into a specific point on
the second toe is said to banish headaches. A needle between
the second and third toe can get rid of a sore throat. A needle
put into the outside of a foot can stimulate vision.

Acupuncture began in China more than four thousand years
ago. It is based on the belief that there is a natural flow of energy
inside each human being. This energy, or life force, is called *qi*
(pronounced CHEE). The qi is said to flow along certain pathways
in the body. These pathways, called meridians, are like rivers.
When they flow freely, you feel strong and healthy. But if one of
your meridians gets blocked, the flow of energy is disrupted. Too
much qi builds up in one part of your body. By inserting needles
in the right spots, specialists can unblock your meridians and get
your qi flowing correctly again.

Words Read
10
23
32
45
49
61
72
83
97
107
116
131
143
154
164
177
188
201
212
217

Needs Work   1   2   3   4   5   Excellent
Paid attention to punctuation

Needs Work   1   2   3   4   5   Excellent
Sounded good

Total Words Read _____

Total Errors − _____

Correct WPM _____

Progress Graph

1. For the first reading of the selection, put a red dot on the line above the selection number to show your correct words-per-minute rate.

2. For the second reading, put a blue dot on the line above the selection number to show your correct words-per-minute rate.

3. Make a graph to show your progress. Connect the red dots from selection to selection with red lines. Connect the blue dots with blue lines.

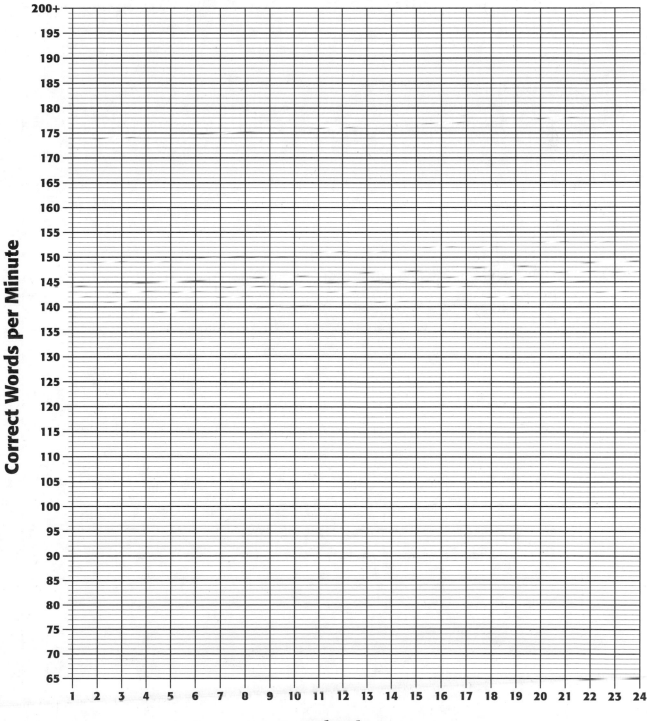

Correct Words per Minute

Selection

Progress Graph

1. For the first reading of the selection, put a red dot on the line above the selection number to show your correct words-per-minute rate.

2. For the second reading, put a blue dot on the line above the selection number to show your correct words-per-minute rate.

3. Make a graph to show your progress. Connect the red dots from selection to selection with red lines. Connect the blue dots with blue lines.

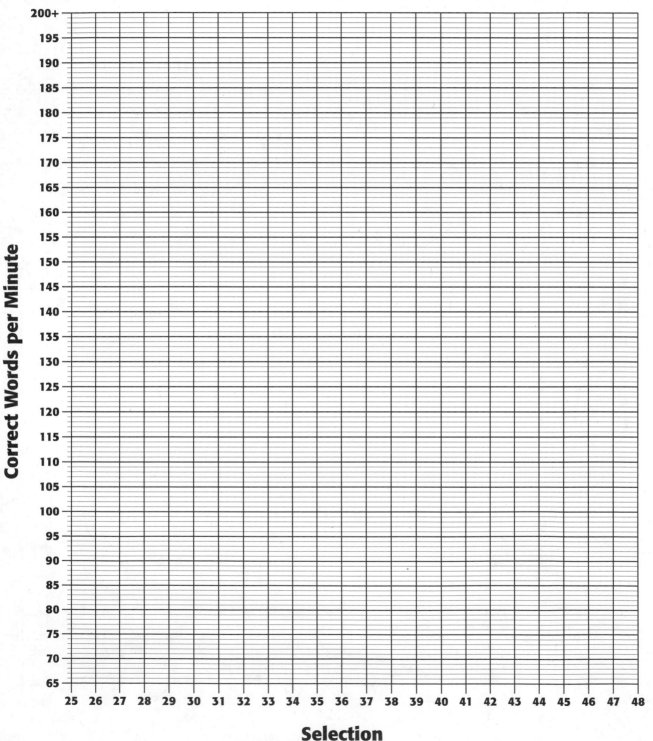

Correct Words per Minute

200+
195
190
185
180
175
170
165
160
155
150
145
140
135
130
125
120
115
110
105
100
95
90
85
80
75
70
65

25 26 27 28 29 30 31 32 33 34 35 36 37 38 39 40 41 42 43 44 45 46 47 48

Selection

Progress Graph

1. For the first reading of the selection, put a red dot on the line above the selection number to show your correct words-per-minute rate.

2. For the second reading, put a blue dot on the line above the selection number to show your correct words-per-minute rate.

3. Make a graph to show your progress. Connect the red dots from selection to selection with red lines. Connect the blue dots with blue lines.

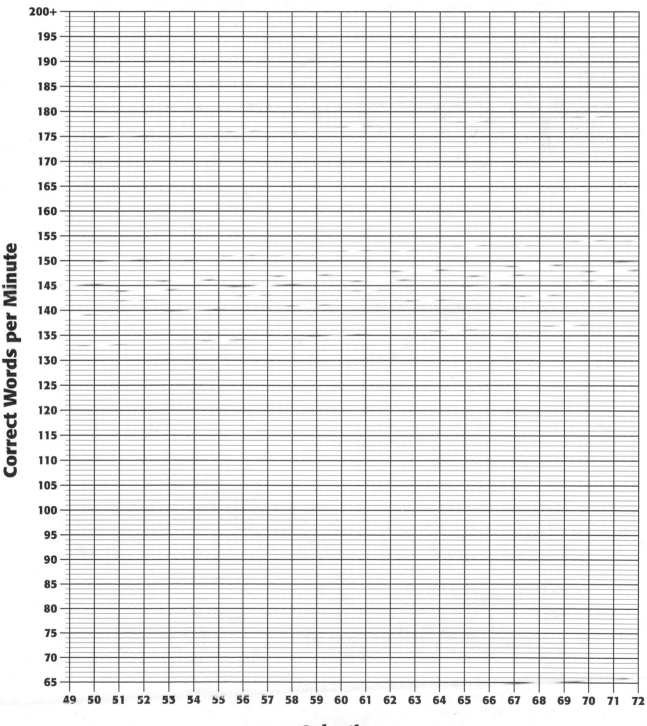

Correct Words per Minute

Selection

Acknowledgments

Grateful acknowledgment is given to the authors and publishers listed below for brief passages excerpted from these longer works.

from "The Summer of the Beautiful White Horse" from *My Name Is Aram* by William Saroyan. Copyright © 1937, 1938, 1939, 1940 and renewed 1966 by William Saroyan. Harcourt Brace & World.

from *Where the Red Fern Grows* by Wilson Rawls. Copyright © 1961 by Woodrow Wilson Rawls; copyright © 1961 by The Curtis Publishing Company. Random House Children's Books, a division of Random House.

from *The Secret Garden* by Frances Hodgson Burnett. Copyright © 1987 by Dell Yearling, a division of Bantam Doubleday Dell Publishing Group.

from *On My Honor* by Marion Dane Bauer. Copyright © 1986 by Marion Dane Bauer. Clarion Books/Ticknor & Fields, Houghton Mifflin.

from *Pioneer Girl: Growing Up on the Prairie* by Andrea Warren. Copyright © 1998 by Andrea Warren. Morrow Junior Books, a division of William Morrow and Company.

from *Out of Darkness: The Story of Louis Braille* by Russell Freedman. Copyright © 1997 by Russell Freedman. Clarion Books, an imprint of Houghton Mifflin.

from *Living up the Street: Narrative Reflections* by Gary Soto. Copyright © 1985 by Gary Soto. Bantam Doubleday Dell Publishing Group.

from *My Indian Boyhood* by Luther Standing Bear. Copyright © 1931 by Luther Standing Bear and renewed 1959 by May M. Jones. University of Nebraska Press.

from *The Dolphins and Me* by Don C. Reed. Copyright © 1989 by Don C. Reed. Sierra Club Books/Little, Brown.

from *Old Yeller* by Fred Gipson. Copyright © 1956 by Fred Gipson. Harper & Row.

from *First in Their Hearts: A Biography of George Washington* by Thomas Fleming. Copyright © 1967, 1968, 1984 by Thomas Fleming. Walker and Company.

from *Gone-Away Lake* by Elizabeth Enright. Copyright © 1957 by Elizabeth Enright. Harcourt, Brace & World.

from *Dust Tracks on a Road* by Zora Neale Hurston. Copyright © 1942 by Zora Neale Hurston and renewed 1970 by John C. Hurston. HarperCollins Publishers.

from *Making Headlines: A Biography of Nellie Bly* by Kathy Lynn Emerson. Copyright © 1989 by Dillon Press.

from "The Stone and the Cross" by Ciro Alegría, translated by Zoila Nelken and Rosalie Torres-Rioseco. In *Short Stories of Latin America,* ed. Arturo Torres-Rioseco. Copyright © 1963 by Las Americas Publishing Company.

from "Through the Tunnel" from *The Habit of Loving* by Doris Lessing. Copyright © 1954, 1955 by Doris Lessing. HarperCollins Publishers. Originally appeared in the *New Yorker*. Copyright renewed.

from "Rules of the Game" from *The Joy Luck Club* by Amy Tan. Copyright © 1989 by Amy Tan. Putnam Berkley, a division of Penguin Putnam.

from *Le Morte d'Arthur* by Sir Thomas Malory, translated by Keith Baines. Copyright © 1967 by Keith Baines. Clarkson M. Potter, a division of Crown Publishers.

from *Hiding to Survive* by Maxine B. Rosenberg. Copyright © 1994 by Maxine B. Rosenberg. Clarion Books, an imprint of Houghton Mifflin.

from "Neighbor Rosicky" from *Obscure Destinies* by Willa Cather. Copyright © 1930, 1932 by Willa Cather and renewed 1958, 1960 by the executors of the estate of Willa Cather. Vintage Books, a division of Random House. Originally published by Alfred A. Knopf, 1932.

from "The Old Demon" by Pearl S. Buck, 1939. Copyright © 1939 and renewed 1966 by Pearl S. Buck.

from *Rosa Parks: My Story* by Rosa Parks with Jim Haskins. Copyright © 1992 by Rosa Parks. Dial Books for Young Readers, a division of Penguin Putnam.

from *Banner in the Sky* by James Ramsey Ullman. Copyright © 1954 by James Ramsey Ullman. Harper Keypoint, a division of Harper & Row.

from "Another April" from *The Best-Loved Short Stories of Jesse Stuart*. Copyright © 1982 by the Jesse Stuart Foundation. McGraw-Hill.

from *Growing Up* by Russell Baker. Copyright © 1982 by Russell Baker. Congdon & Weed.

from *So Far from the Bamboo Grove* by Yoko Kawashima Watkins. Copyright © 1986 by Yoko Kawashima Watkins. Lothrop, Lee & Shepard Books, a division of William Morrow.

from *Julie of the Wolves* by Jean Craighead George. Copyright © 1972 by Jean Craighead George. HarperCollins Publishers.